Holiday Patterns

ROUTER

ROTARY TOOL

SCROLL SAW

Patrick and Patricia Spielman

 Sterling Publishing Co., Inc.   New York

Special Edition   Sears 9-25129

Printed July 1992

© 1991 by Patrick & Patricia Spielman
Published by Sterling Publishing Company, Inc.
387 Park Avenue South, New York, N.Y. 10016
Manufactured in the United States of America
All rights reserved

Contents

Color section follows p. 64.

Recommended Power Tool Accessories You Can Use with Patterns

Router

Rout-A-Copier
Model 9 25126
Can be used to engrave
Holiday Patterns in wood
at full size.

Foot Switch
Model 9 25172
Scroll Saw and Router with
Rout-A-Copier are more
enjoyable to use with a
foot-controlled switch.

Rotary

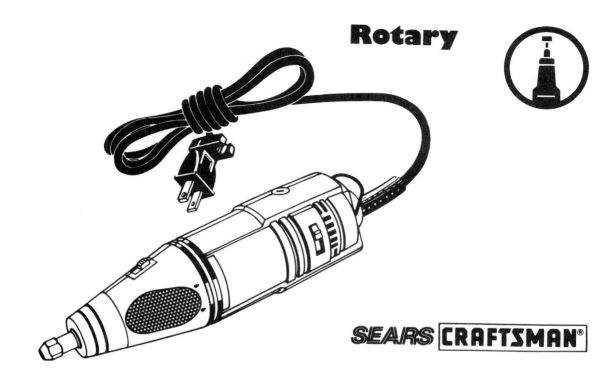

SEARS CRAFTSMAN®

Use to edge small parts— groove or sand	Drill Press Use with rotary tools	Adapts your rotary tool into a router
		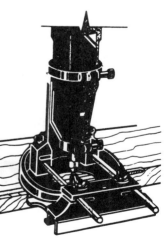
Model 9 53034	Model 9 53032	Model 9 53097

Scroll Saw

Patterns in this book are for use with a scroll saw, and many lend themselves to router operations. Sears has additional patterns available with fret and country themes. Pictured below are a few fretwork patterns from the kit.

Sears Model 9 25066 This kit can be purchased through the Sears Power and Hand Tool Catalog.

Introduction

Scroll Saw Holiday Patterns contains over 300 new, individual designs and projects in nine major categories, providing ready-to-use patterns for most holidays and special family occasions. Most of these patterns are presented in what we think are usable full sizes. However, because individual needs and preferences vary, we hope that you will change the sizes of our patterns or modify them to satisfy your particular needs. For example, small hanging ornaments may be enlarged to make huge lawn-size or yard-size decorations, and conversely some of our larger cutouts can be reduced to make small hanging ornaments. Experiment with several changes of size, as desired.

Sizing, Copying and Transferring Patterns

The easiest and fastest way to enlarge or reduce patterns is with the assistance of a modern office copier machine. If one is not available for your use, there are other methods you can use that have traditionally been used for enlarging drawings, such as using square grids or pantographs.

A copier-machine-enlarged pattern is highly desirable, because it is accurate and it can be applied directly to the wood for the sawing guide (Illus. 1). The copies can be temporarily bonded directly onto the surface of the workpiece using a brush-on rubber cement or a *temporary* bonding spray adhesive (Illus. 2). We prefer the spray-adhesive technique. There are several spray adhesives available that will work, but we recommend a spray mount artist's adhesive such as 3M's Scotch brand. Most photography stores and studios carry this, as do art graphics and craft supply stores. One can will last about a year. It's a great time-saving product.

To use the adhesive, simply spray a very light mist onto the back of the pattern copy—*do not spray on wood*—see Illus. 2. Wait 10 to 30 seconds, press the pattern copy onto your wood (Illus. 3) with hand pressure, and, presto! you're ready to begin sawing—just that easy and just that quick! Gone are the frustrations of doing tracings, working with messy carbon papers, and

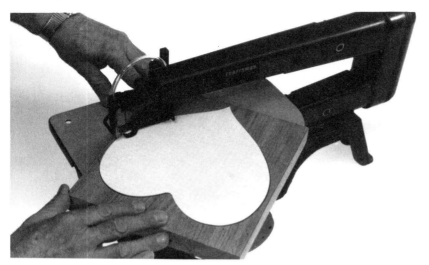

Illus. 1 Any small scroll saw can be used to make most of the projects in this book. Here one-inch-thick wood with a copied pattern applied to it is cut with a narrow blade.

Illus. 2 Apply a very light "mist" of spray adhesive only to the back of the pattern. Do not spray directly onto the wood. Note that a newspaper underneath the pattern is being used to catch the overspray.

Illus. 3 Pressing down a spray-adhesive-coated copy of the pattern directly onto the wood workpiece blank.

similar techniques that never really produced the clear, crisp, accurate layout lines which are so essential to good sawing.

Saw following the same lines of the pattern. When sawing is completed, the pattern is easily peeled off the workpiece (Illus. 4). The adhesive virtually leaves no residue on the wood that might inhibit subsequent finishing. We also recommend that you test the tack qualities of the adhesive to be sure that, at first use, you are spraying just enough for an effective temporary bond, and no more.

If you decide to use the rubber-cement method to bond a machine-copied pattern to the workpiece, a little more care is required. Do not brush on too heavy a coat. If some cement remains on the wood after peeling off the pattern, it can be removed by rubbing it off with your fingers. *Do not use solvents!*

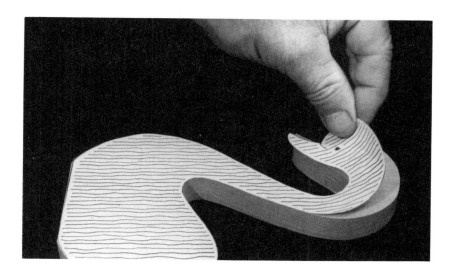

Illus. 4 After sawing is completed, the pattern lifts off the wood easily, leaving no residue to interfere with finishing.

Stack-Sawing Techniques

Stack-sawing involves layering one or more pieces of wood on top of another and sawing them all at once. This technique produces perfectly identical cut pieces and saves time. The layers can be held together in a variety of ways, such as nailing or gluing in the waste areas, using double-faced tape (use very little), wrapping around the stack with masking tape, or stapling the layers together through the waste along the edges. All of the previous ways will work, and certain patterns are better handled with one method than another.

Tip: Use the spray adhesive applied to both sides of strips of paper to make your own double-faced tape. This trick works especially well when stack-sawing thin wood— wood too thin to nail or tack together.

Wood Materials

These patterns can be made from a wide variety of different materials and in a variety of different thicknesses—most of these choices are entirely yours. In some cases we specify or suggest suitable thicknesses where it's important to the visual impact or structural requirements of a particular design. Use cheap soft woods, as a practical choice, if the cutouts are to be coated with opaque finishes. Some of the more highly detailed fretted designs may be best sawn from plywoods that are more durable but sometimes less attractive than solid woods.

Ways to Utilize Patterns

In addition to enlarging or reducing patterns to your own size preferences, there are several ways to individualize patterns (Illus. 5 and 6). Wall-hanging designs can be made into utility projects by adding pegs or hooks to hang various things on. Standing designs can be converted to door stops simply by nailing a thin wedge to the back side. Glue on magnets to make refrigerator-type note holders. Use designs as overlay decorations on boxes, clocks, signs, furniture, and various household accessories. Hang ornaments and/or stand cutouts in windows. Attach metal findings to the backs of minicutouts with epoxy glue to make jewelry. Add glued-on bows, lace, and pieces of fabric to give personality and color to otherwise bland cutouts.

In addition to scroll-sawing out the pattern shapes given in this book, you will find that many patterns lend themselves to bandsawing and several router operations. One very easy but also a very effective technique is to simply round over the outside edges of a cutout using a router with a bit of the desired radius. See Illus. 5, which shows two projects in which the sawn-out segments were rounded over with a router to give a more sculptured, artistic look.

When rounding over small parts or pieces, employ these two techniques: First, replace the existing plastic sub-base of your router with another one that you can make yourself from ⅛- to ¼-inch-thick plastic or plywood. Make it with minimal clearance around the bit (Illus. 6). Thus, you always have the router sufficiently supported on the work piece even if it is relatively small in size. Second, it will be impossible to hold down very small work

Illus. 5. Most all of the parts for these two projects have the edges rounded over with a router.

pieces with any kind of mechanical clamping device. Use double-faced tape or temporarily bond the part to be routed to the workbench with a dab of hot-melt glue. The best method is to just place the work piece on one of the new, popular foam routing pads that are available.

With these new pads the work will not slip or kick out from under the router (Illus. 7).

Many simple profile shapes can be utilized to make projects for specific uses (Illus. 8). Enlarge or reduce patterns as desired.

Illus. 6. This self-made replacement sub-base has minimal open space around the round-over bit.

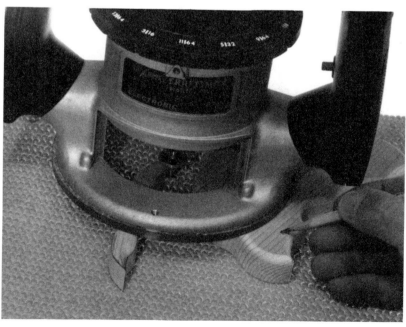

Illus. 7. Here the mustache for the Santa project (Illus. 5) is being rounded over at the edges. Note that this part is kept in place with the router pad under it. Another part of the project is positioned to help keep the router from tipping.

Illus. 8. Many pattern profiles are ideal for making into routed trays. Here a simple heart and Christmas tree profile have central areas routed away to make special holiday snack, candy, or nut trays.

Finishing Cutouts

There are lots of ways and different materials to finish your holiday cutout decorations and ornaments (Illus. 9). Natural finishes, stains, and paints are all good, with your choice a matter of personal preference. Many patterns have lines on the "face" of cutouts to give them personality or character. Lines representing eyes,

Illus. 9. One pattern made in three different ways. Left to right: wood-burned line detailing, painted, and segmented, in which each individual part is cut free, stained (or painted) a different color and reassembled (glued) together to make the object whole again.

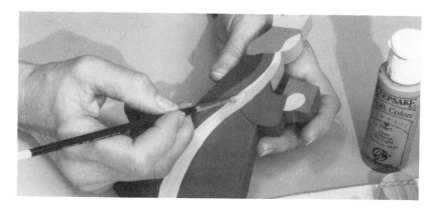

Illus. 10. Use colorful paints for pattern details.

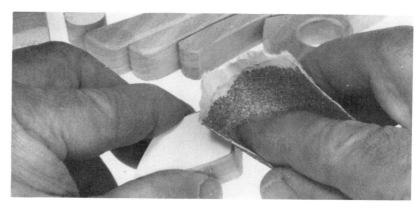

Illus. 11. Wood-burning pattern line details. Using a metal straightedge guide may be helpful.

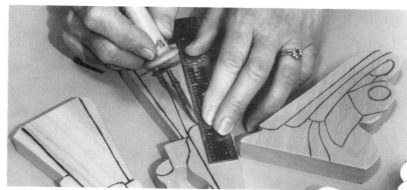

Illus. 12. Slightly rounding over the sawn edges of all segmented pieces. Here a folded piece of 60- or 80-grit abrasive sandpaper is flexed to match and sand an inside curved edge.

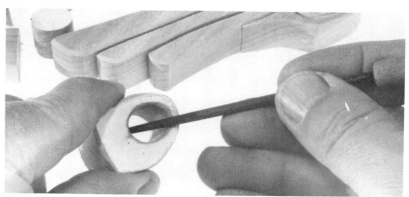

Illus. 13. Use a small file to round edges in tight areas.

mouth, clothes, and the like can be painted (Illus. 10) or wood-burned (Illus. 11)—whatever is in line with your artistic inclinations.

Some small patterns lend themselves well to *segmentation*. This is where lines of the pattern that suggest certain expressive features are cut apart (into segments). All sawn edges of very small parts are rounded slightly, using sandpaper pads (Illus. 12) or files (Illus. 13).

The individual pieces (segments) are put back together again (Illus. 14) prior to being stained or painted (Illus. 15 and see also Illus. 5). Glue the segments to each other to make the whole.

If scroll-sawings and router work are new for you, we recommend you consult the full line of Sears Books.

Illus. 14. Checking the sanded edges of this segmented project with a trial assembly.

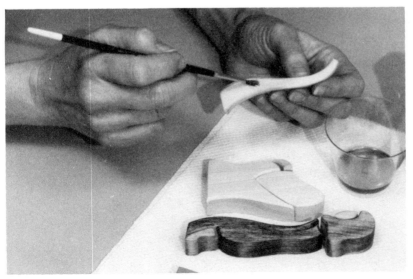

Illus. 15. Segmentation can also incorporate the combination of natural, stained, and painted pieces as desired. Leave inside gluing edges unfinished.

Decorative Valentine "thought" sawn from thin plywood and painted red and white.

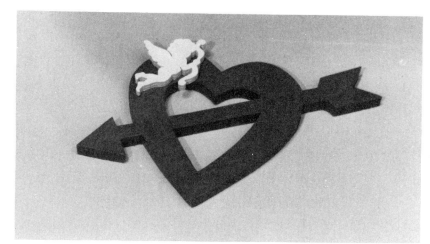

Cutouts in one-inch natural soft maple accented with red painted hearts.

Heart made from ½"-thick plywood with a ¼"-thick plywood overlay.

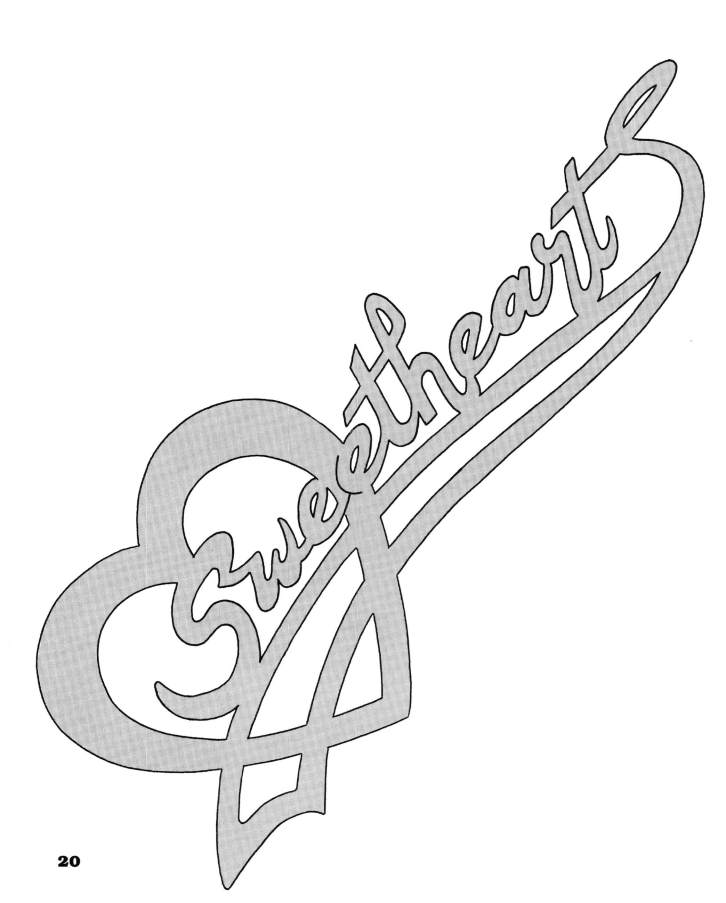

Be my Valentine

Single-heart design, by John Polhemus.

A B C D E F G H I
J K L M N O P Q
R S T U V W X
Y Z 1 2 3 4 5 6
7 8 9 0

Basic-alphabet pattern.

Pattern, courtesy of Kirk Ratajesak.

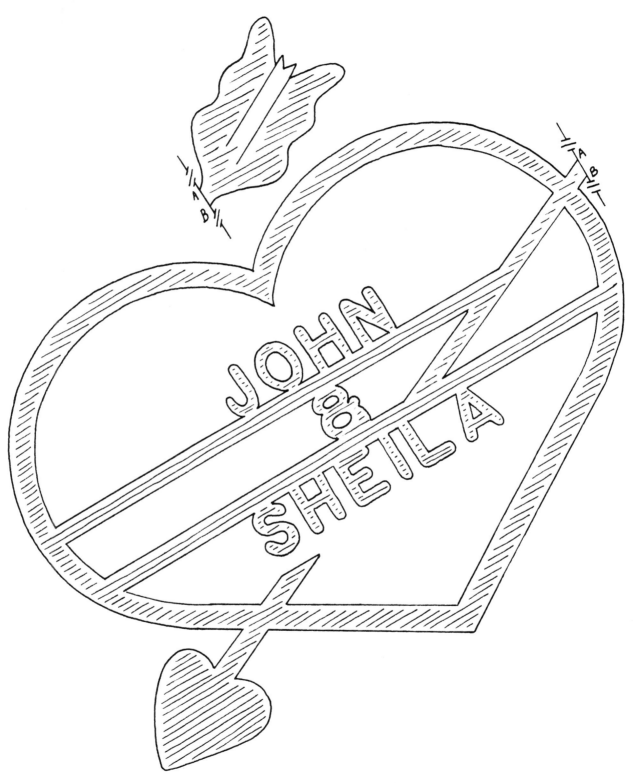

Single heart and arrow, designed by John Polhemus.

Simple heart cutouts can be enhanced by any combination of silk flowers, ribbon, or lace, glued-on with hot-melt adhesive.

Heart cutouts made from ⅝″ to ¾″ solid wood with rounded edges and lace glued to back. Heart design, above right, is cut from ¼″ plywood.

Ornaments can be sawn from any stock from ⅛″ to ½″ thick.

Routing Heart Trays

There are several alternate procedures that can be employed to make the heart tray shown in the photo and similar tray projects. The best procedure to use will depend upon the quantity you intend to make. Will it be just one tray or several, and perhaps more made for gifts or as products to sell? The best technique also hinges on the style of router bits in your collection. The rounded inside corner of the tray's recess can be cut with a core box bit. Then, follow this with a straight-cutting bit to remove the inside area and make the bottom flat and the walls vertically straight.

Or, special combination bits are available that will cut the inside radius, make a flat bottoming cut and a straight wall all at once. See the photo of the special bit. A template guide bushing can also be used to guide the router along the template when bits without mounted ball-bearing guides are used. See the photos of the guide bushing and the single combination tray bit.

This next photo shows a router with a larger base mounted to it. A base such as this is especially helpful in that the base bridges across the template opening. This technique assures that the router will not tip downward into the template opening, making a deeper bottoming cut than desired. See also the last photo.

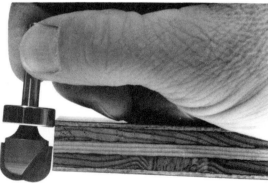

This routed heart tray requires making a template to guide the router.

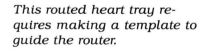

This special bit is designed for routing trays. Note that it is guided against the template by a ball-bearing guide on the shank.

Use a Sears guide bushing mounted to your router base when using bits without mounted guide bearings. The outside of the bushing follows the edge of the tray template.

Use the single combination tray bit as shown (without the ball-bearing guide) or use two separate bits; i.e., a core box and a straight bit. All bits must be of a smaller cutting diameter than the inside opening of the guide bushing.

A router with an extended base and a ball-bearing guided tray bit.

With the template tacked in the corners (with headless nails) to the work piece, rout out the inside area. Note the work is being done on a router pad, eliminating the need for clamps. Finally, saw the outside profile and use the router again to round over all outside edges.

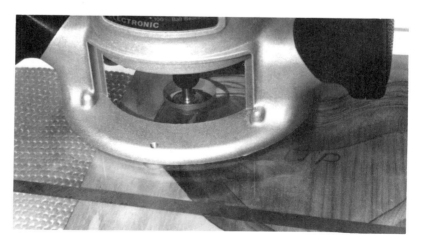

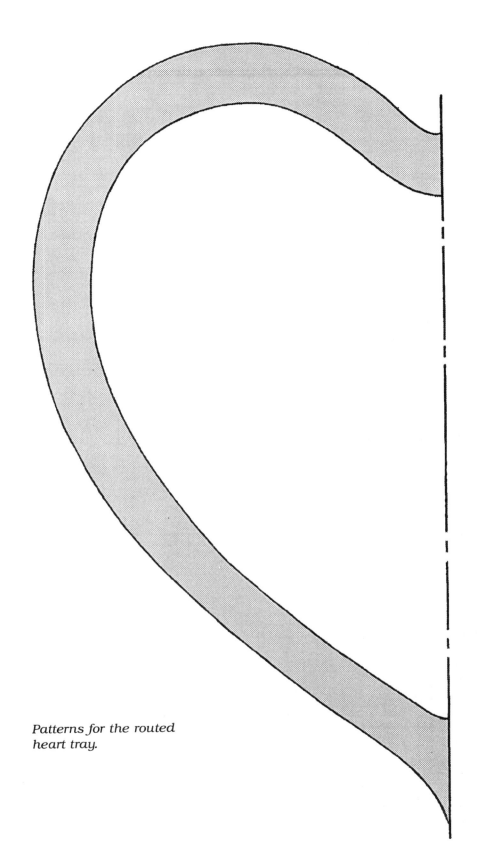

*Patterns for the routed
heart tray.*

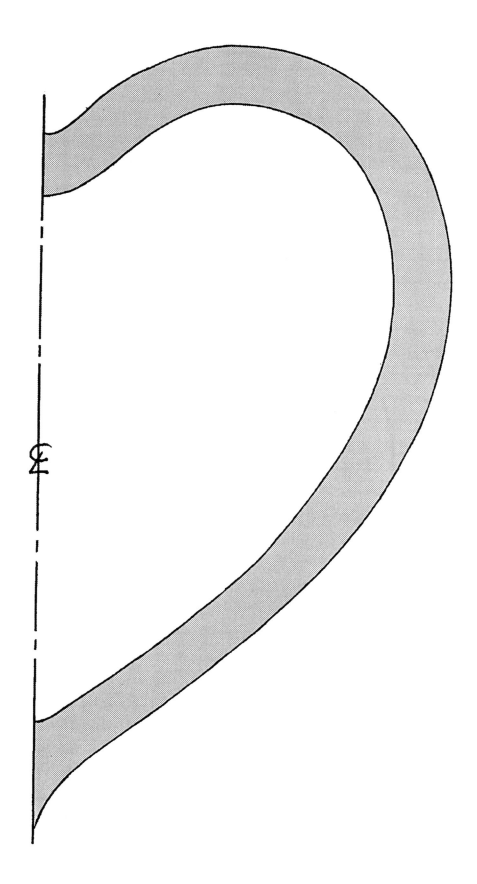

St. Patrick's Day

A standing shamrock for St. Pat's Day is sawn from any material at least ¾" thick.

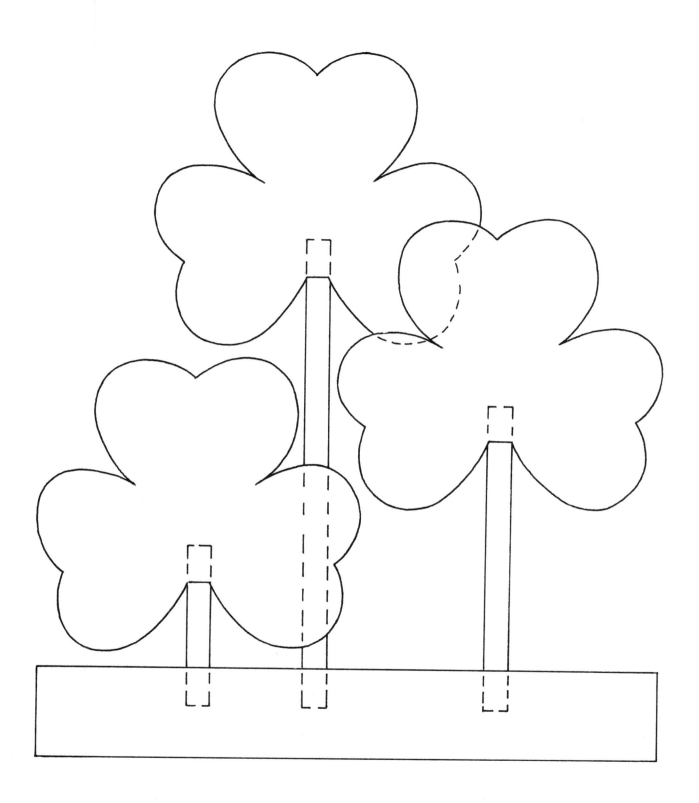

Standing bunny on the left has colorful pants of fabric applied with glue along with other painted details. Bunny on the right combines fretwork and painted detailing.

Easter design in ¾"-thick unfinished poplar.

Rocking bunny sawn from ¾"-thick and ½"-thick material decorated with paint, ribbon, and glued-on cotton tail.

50

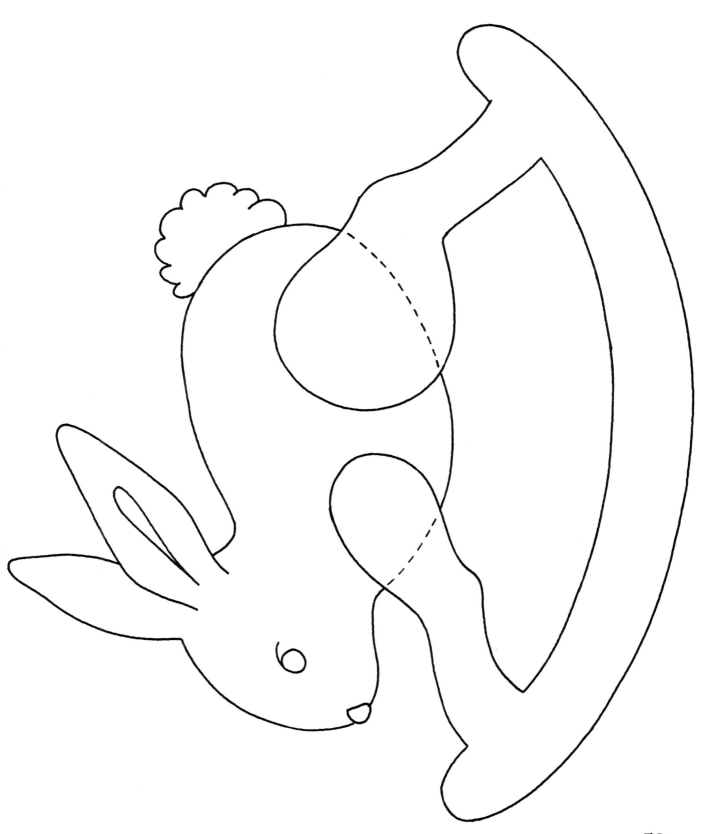

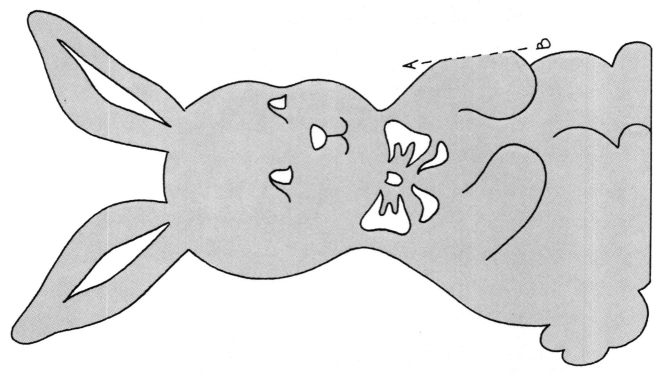

A

B

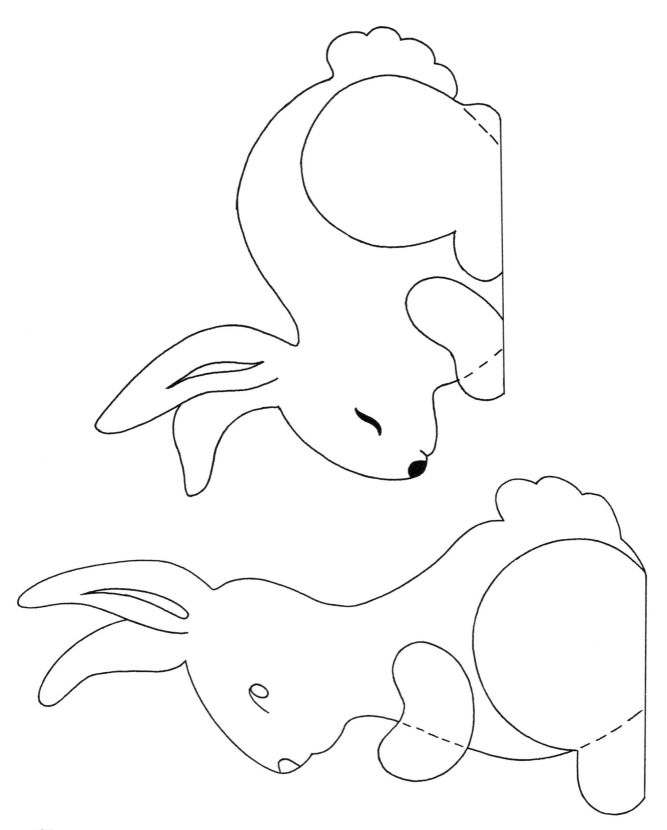

Dimensional bunnies made from ¾"-thick and ½"-thick material. Note the colorful ribbon used for the final decorative touch.

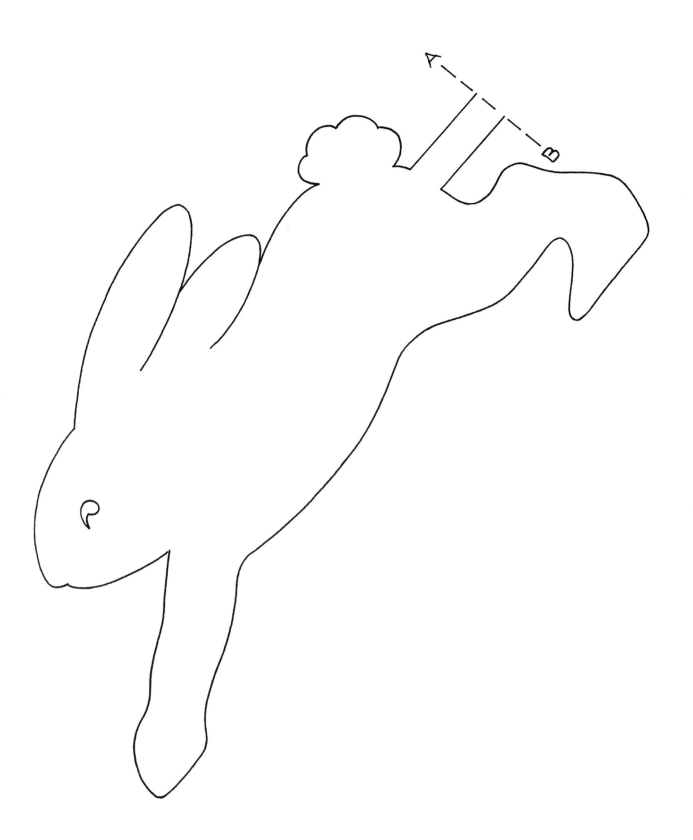

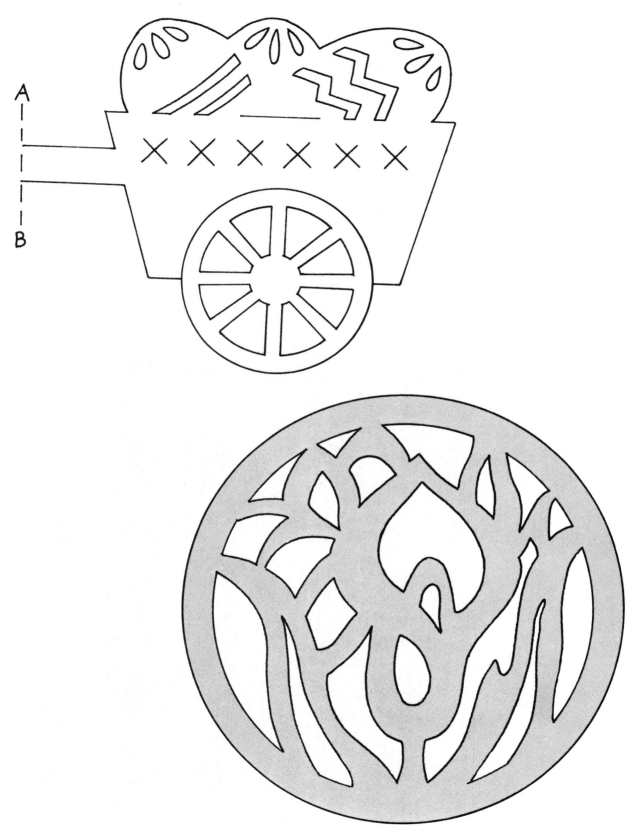

A

B

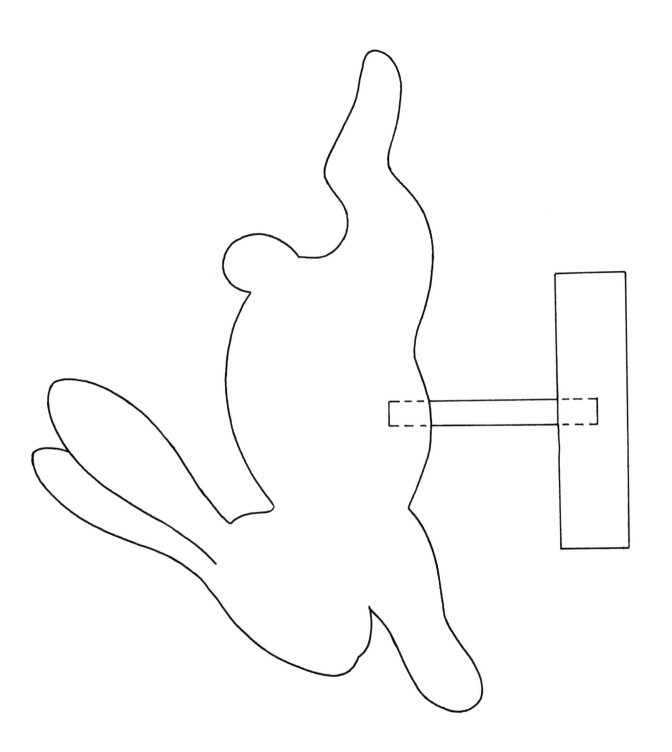

A family of ghosts and other fun cutouts for Halloween.

A variety of Christmas fretwork sawn from birch plywood, left unfinished.

Painted cutouts, ¾"- to 1½"-thick material can be used.

A group of painted Christmas decorations.

Painted nativity set.

Nativity set characters made by the segmenting technique, with oil-stained colorization.

A variety of delicate, fretted ornaments made from thin domestic and exotic woods.

Wall hanging and standing Christmas decorations. The two at the right can also be used as trivets.

A variety of delicate, fretted ornaments made from thin domestic and exotic wood.

D

Fretwork Easter decorations sawn from ¾" mahogany, with natural oil finish.

A variety of delicate, fretted ornaments made from thin domestic and exotic woods.

Fretwork Easter decorations sawn from ¾" mahogany, with natural oil finish.

E

Make these painted ornaments from material ¼" or less in thickness.

A shamrock among cutouts for Valentine's Day.

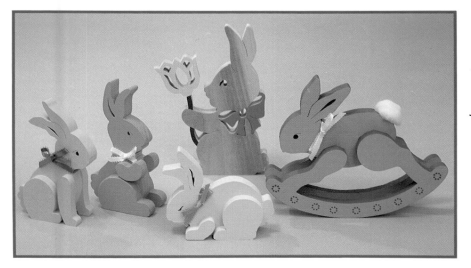

Variety of projects made from ¾"- and ½"-thick wood, painted, with ribbon and cotton used for interesting finishing touches.

Colorful Thanksgiving cutouts.

Christmas decorations made of ¾"-thick painted wood. Dimensional trees sawn from ¼"-thick material.

An ornament tree for any holiday, with interchangeable treetop designs.

These cutouts, a fretted pumpkin and solid cat, make an interesting combination.

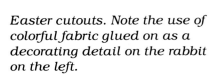

Easter cutouts. Note the use of colorful fabric glued on as a decorating detail on the rabbit on the left.

H

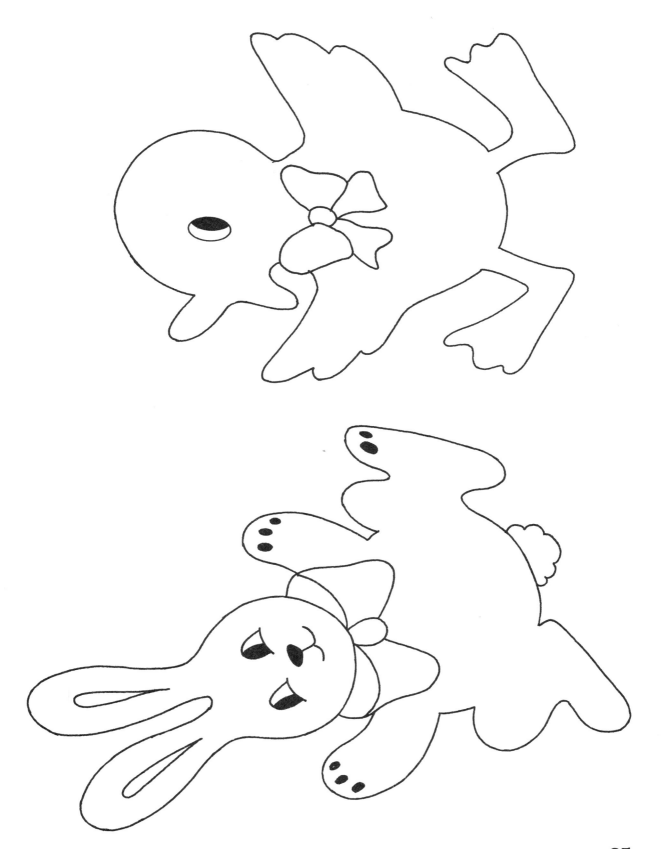

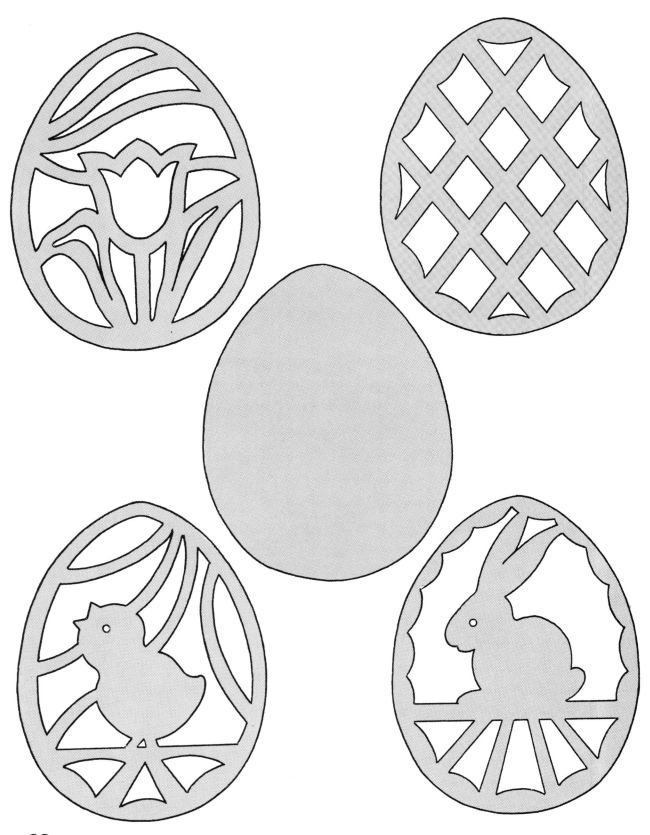

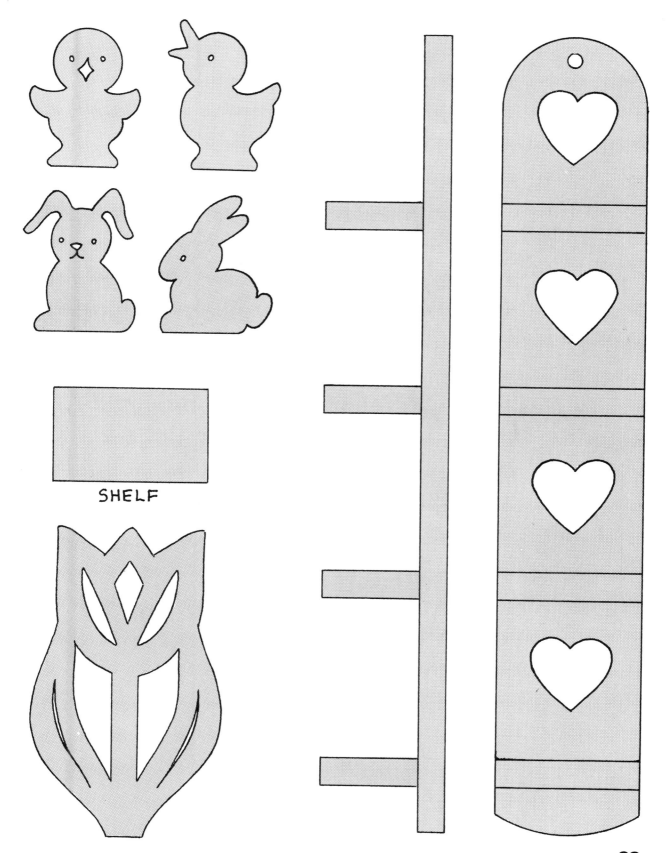

SHELF

Cross sawn from ¾-inch-thick mahogany.

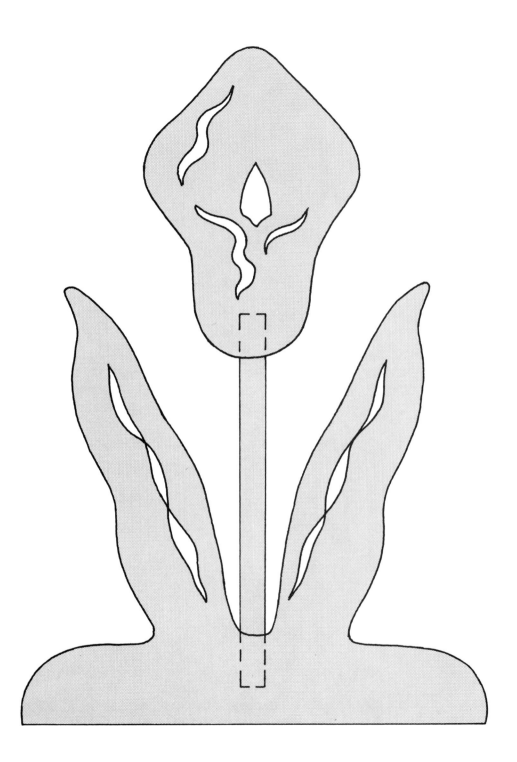

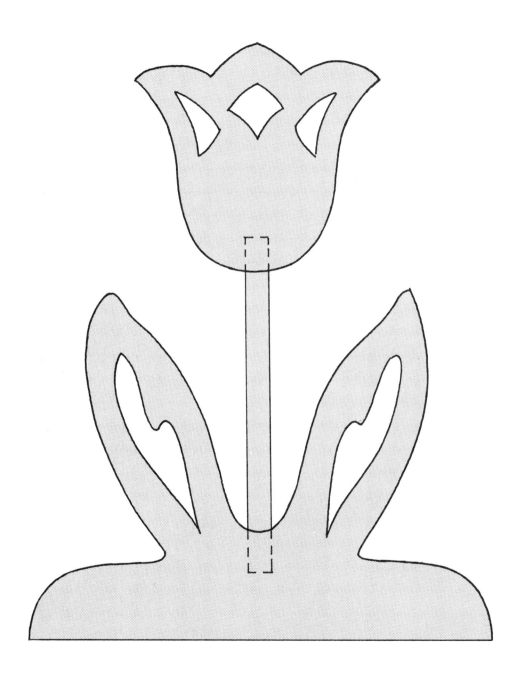

Easter egg cutout sawn from mahogany, ³/₄" thick.

Fretted Easter design cut from ³/₄"-thick mahogany.

80

82

84

85

90

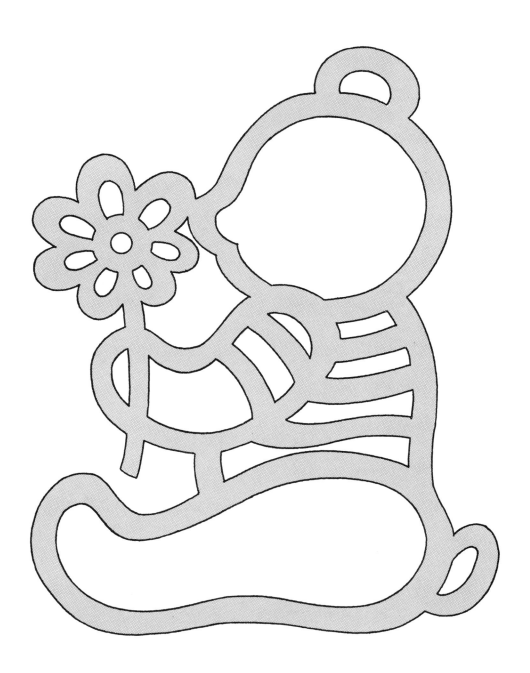

Patriotic Holidays

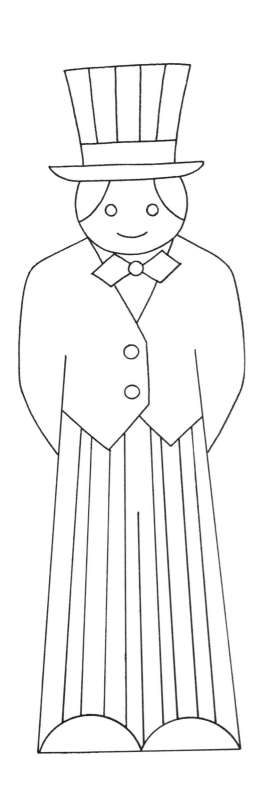

97

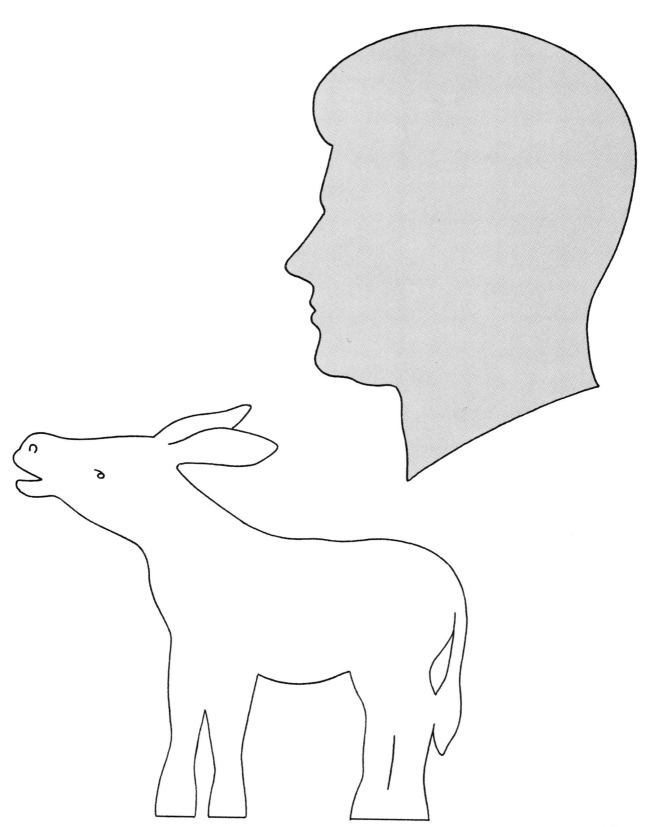

101

Halloween

Painted pine cutouts.

103

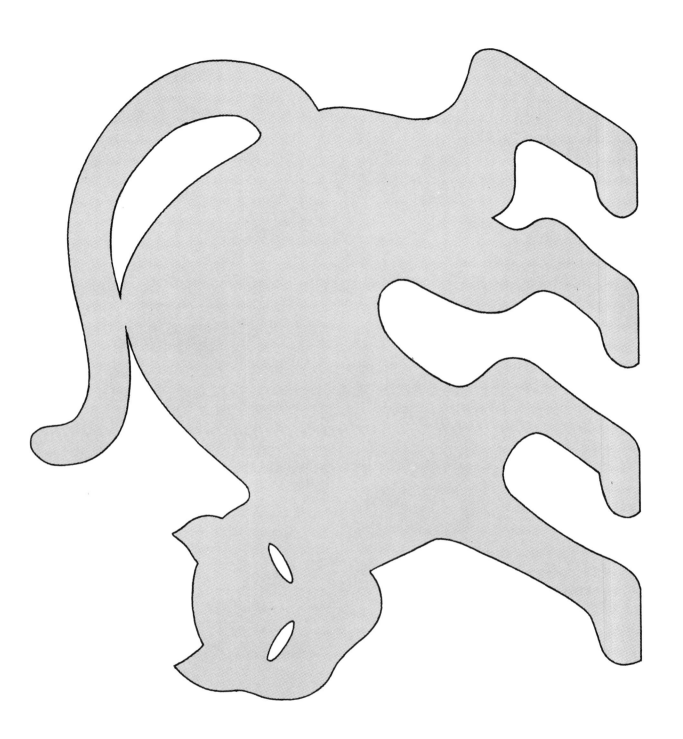

Halloween cat. Cut from two pieces of ¾-inch-thick pine. Round over the edges, as shown, with a router. Apply dark stain and sand the edges with abrasive on a flat block to create the randomly lightened edges, as shown.

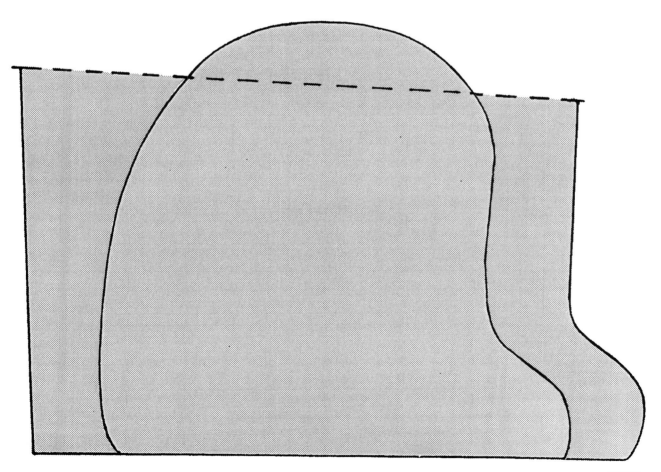

114

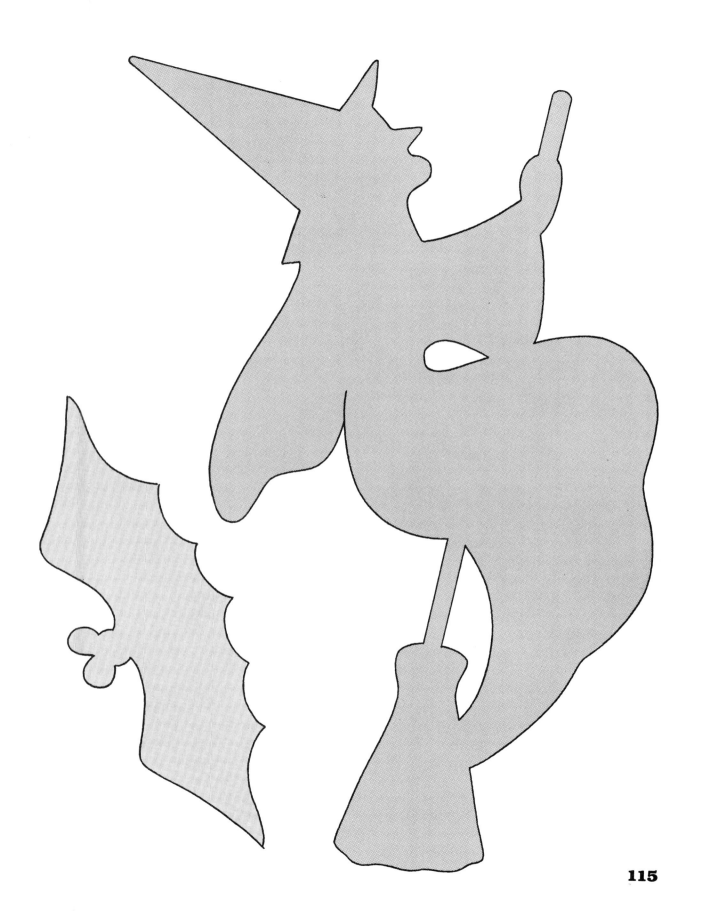

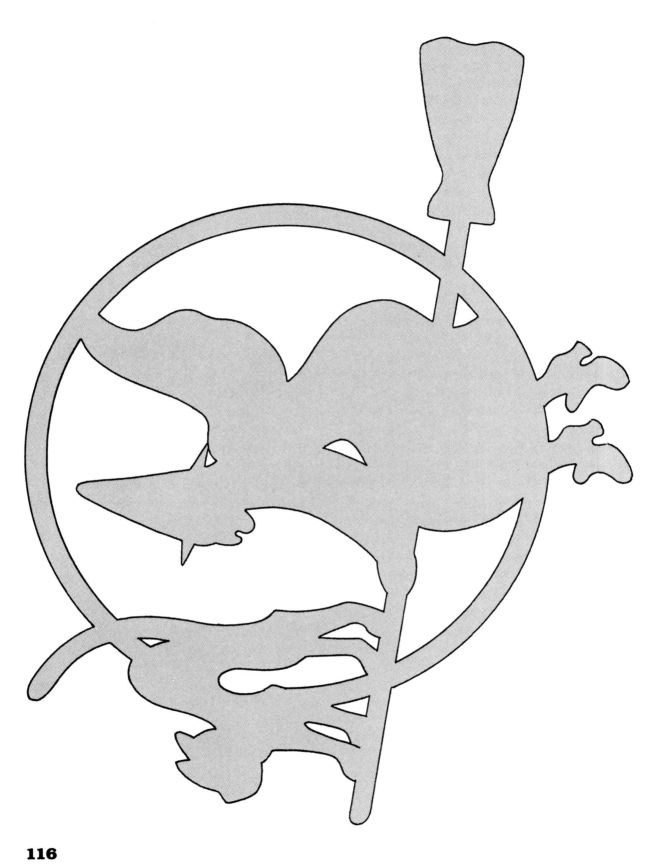

116

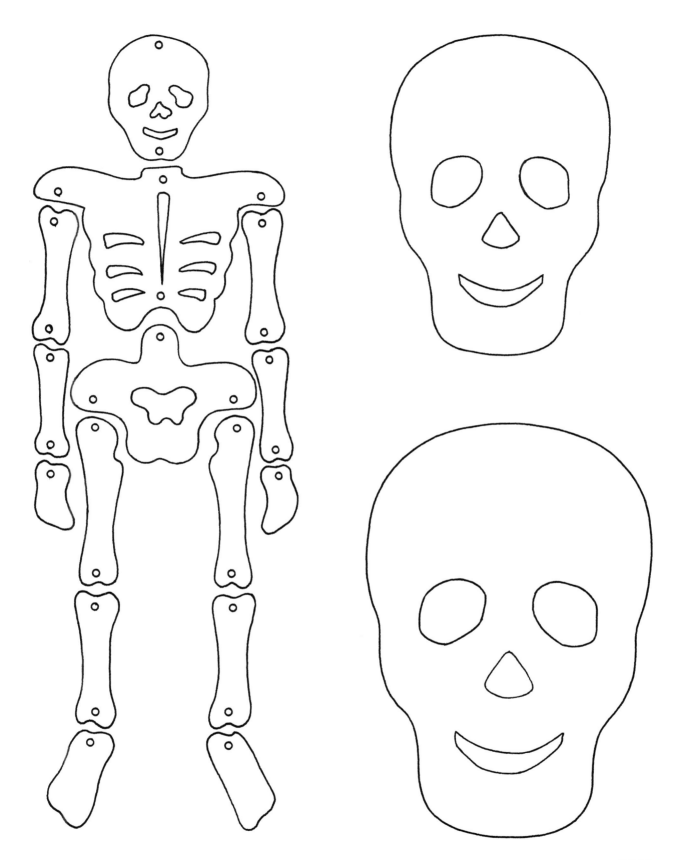

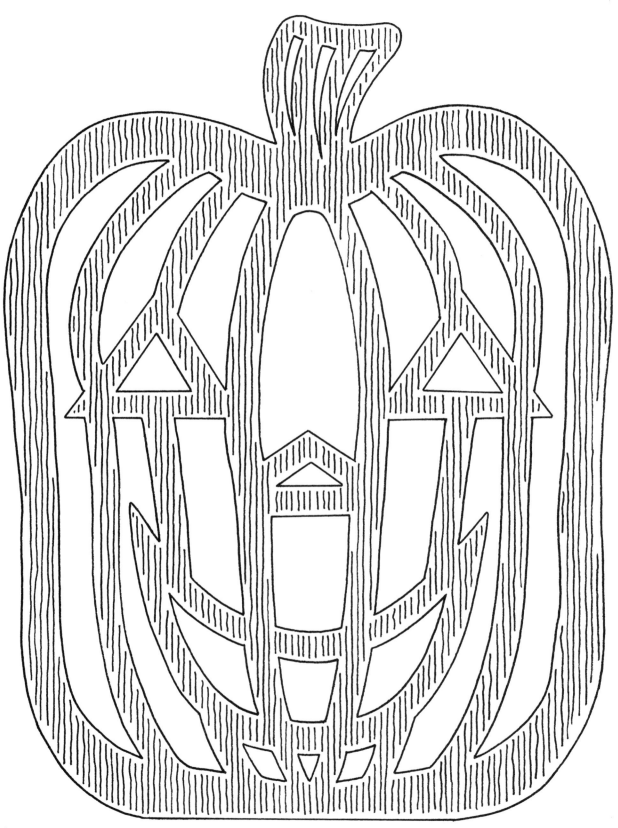

118

Thanksgiving

Thanksgiving cutouts made from ¾"-thick painted softwood with ½"-thick material used for the turkey wings.

123

124

Segmented characters for the Nativity set.

Painted Nativity set.

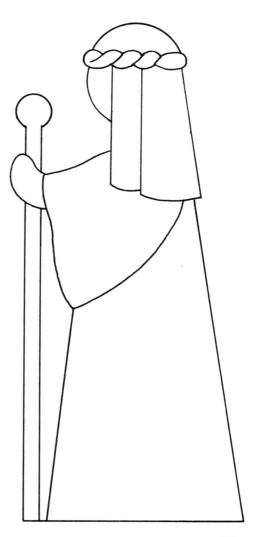

127

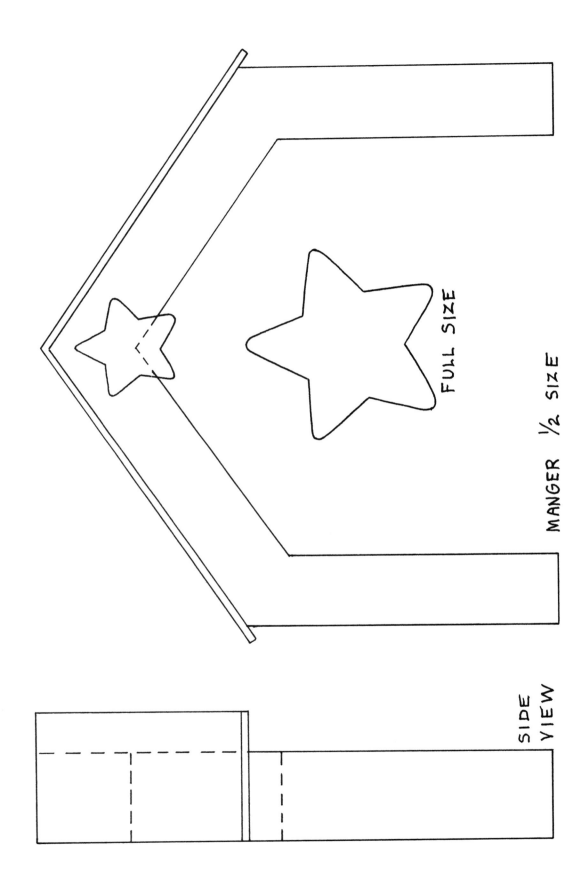

FULL SIZE

MANGER ½ SIZE

SIDE
VIEW

130

133

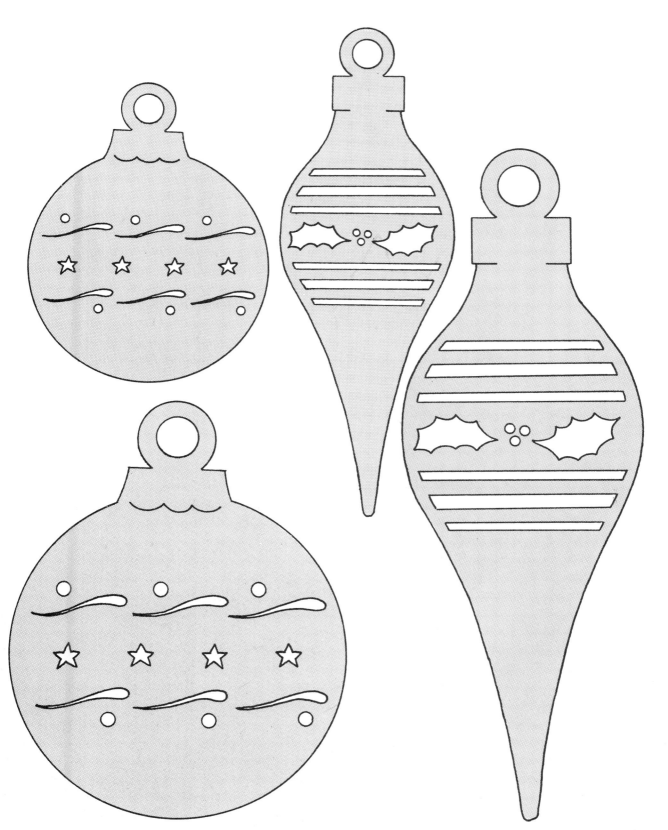

138

Snowman family cut from ³⁄₄"-thick material and painted.

Mr. and Mrs. Santa sawn from ³⁄₄"-thick material and painted.

Pair of Santas sawn from ³⁄₄"-thick material.

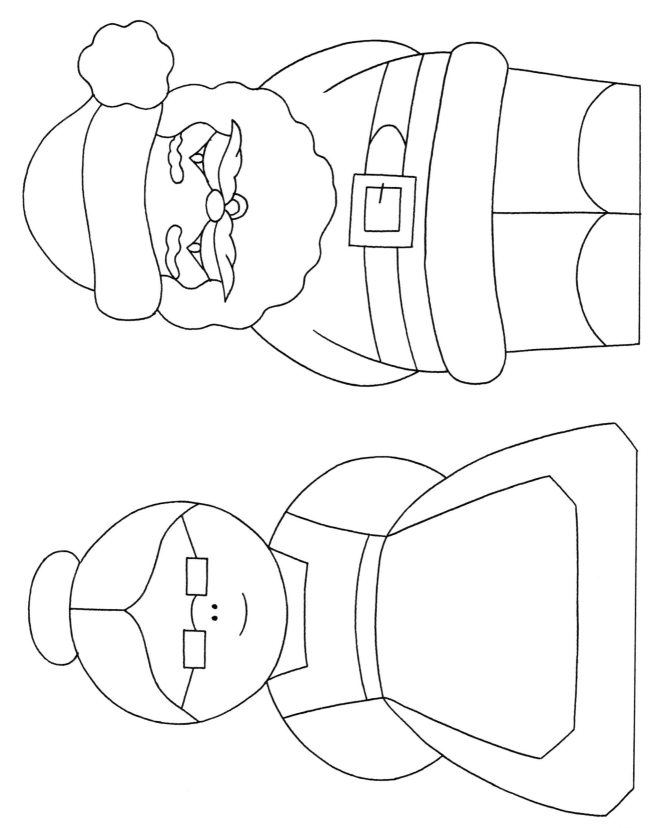

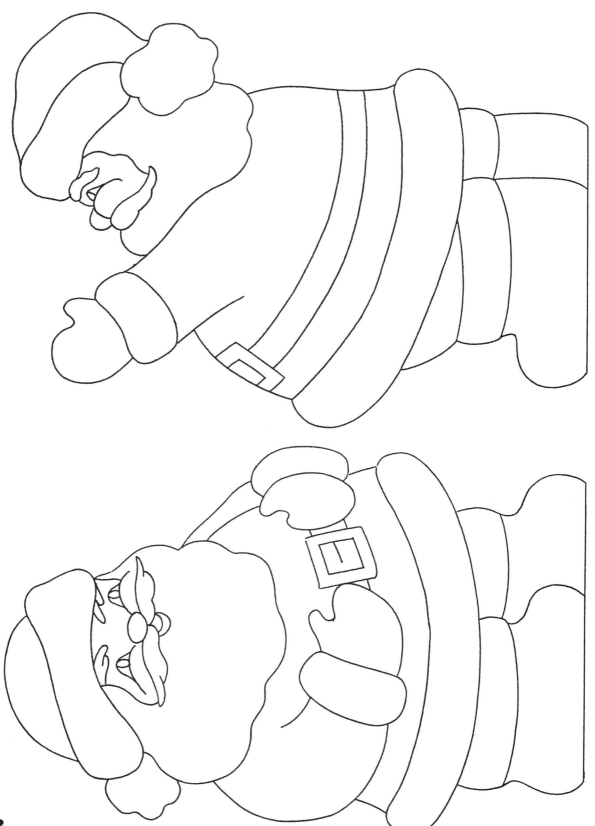

142

Trees at left, ¾" thick. Dimensional trees at right made from ¼"-thick stock.

Trees, 1½" thick, and ¾"-thick angel with plain antique finish.

Wreath, ¾" thick, with ⅜"-thick bow overlay.

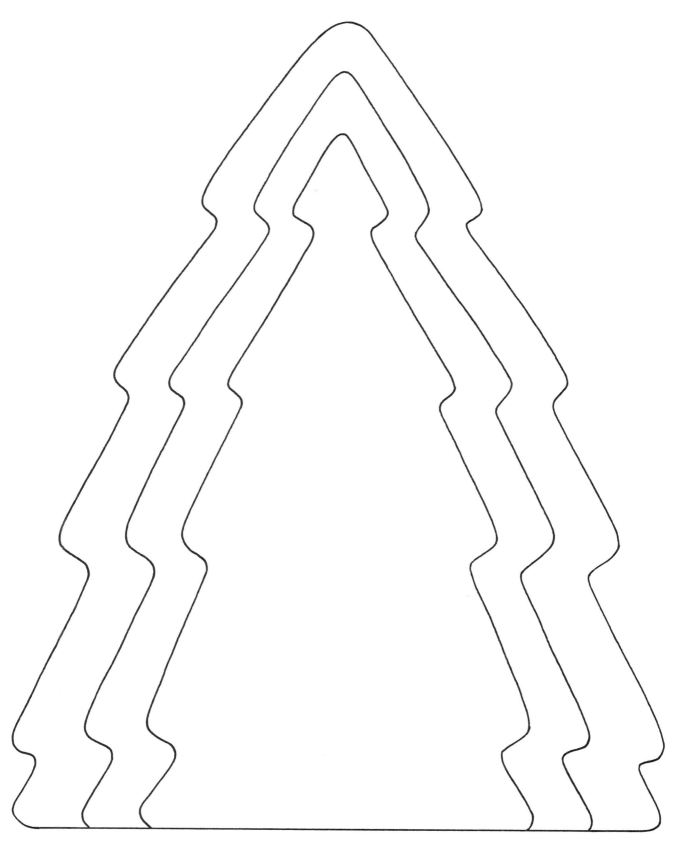

*Circular dashed line indicates optional back
rabbet cut for use as a picture frame.*

Base, ¼″ × 2¼″ × 4½″.

A

A

B

B

149

Trees and horse, ¾″ thick, with antique finish.

150

Rocking horse sawn from ¾"-thick and ½"-thick softwood, painted with darker edges.

151

152

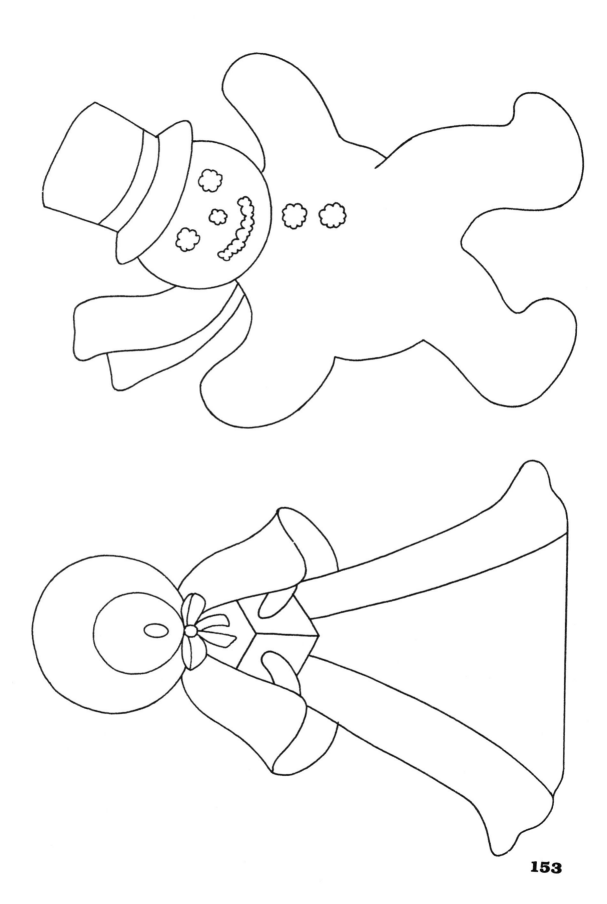

153

155

156

Cut out letters in pine ¾ inch thick. Note: All outside edges should be rounded over using a ⅜-inch-radius corner-rounding bit.

Rounding over the outside edges. A ⅜-inch corner-rounding bit is used with a special self-made router base, and the routing pad, as shown, permits routing the work pieces without clamping.

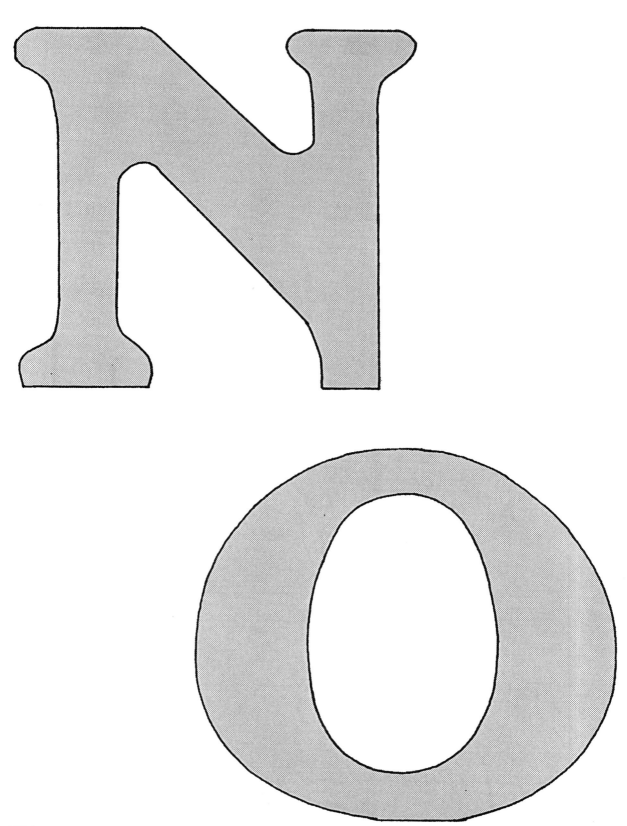

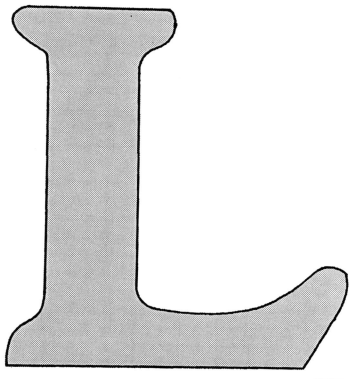

159

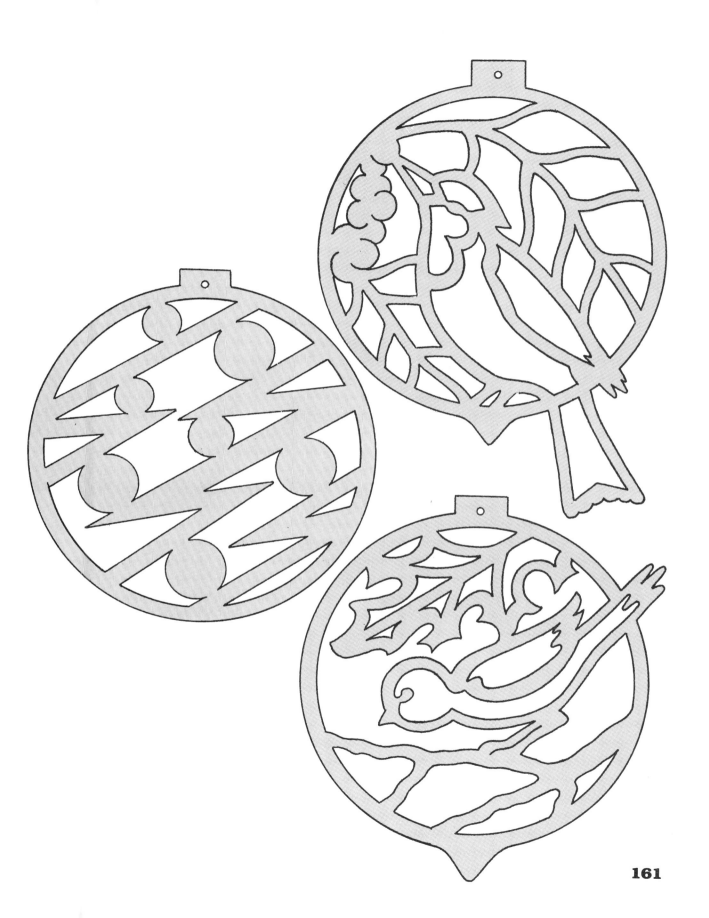

Fretwork angel. Cut from any suitable material.

Unfinished plywood, ¼″ thick, was used for this cutout.

This plywood cutout can be made from any thickness material and can either be painted or left unfinished.

Plywood, ¼″ thick, was used for this cutout.

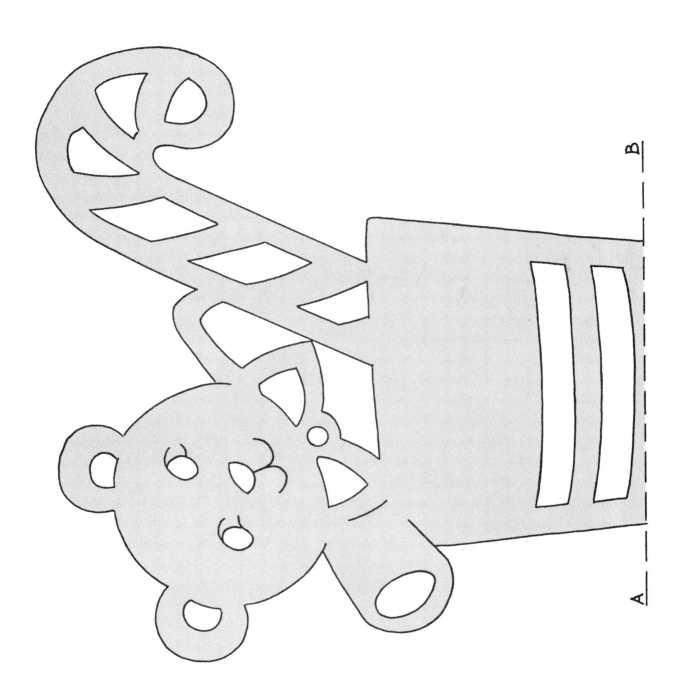

A

B

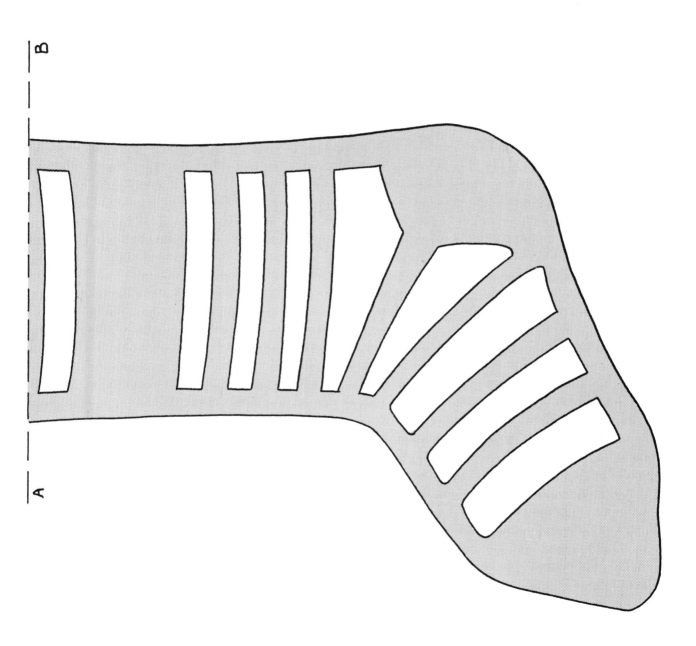

A

B

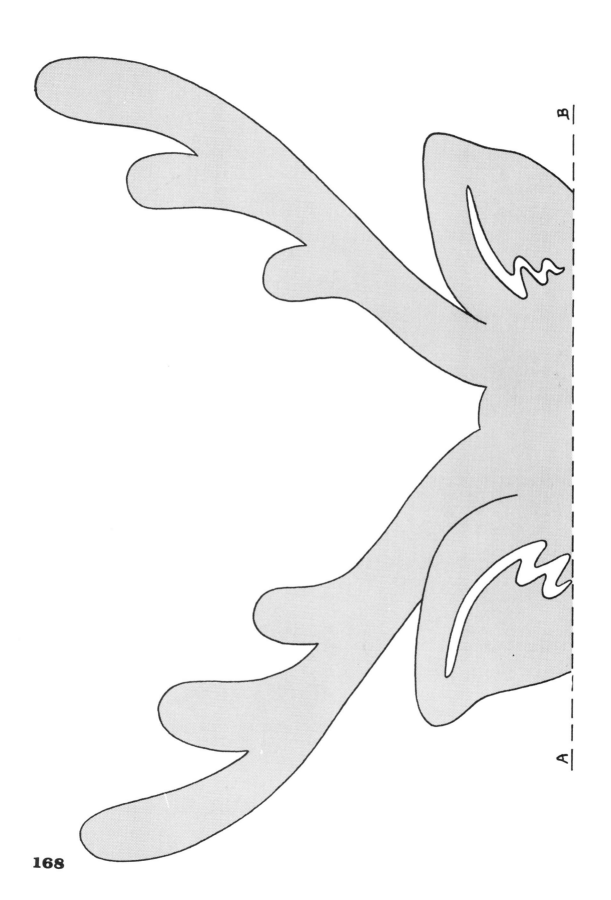

A

B

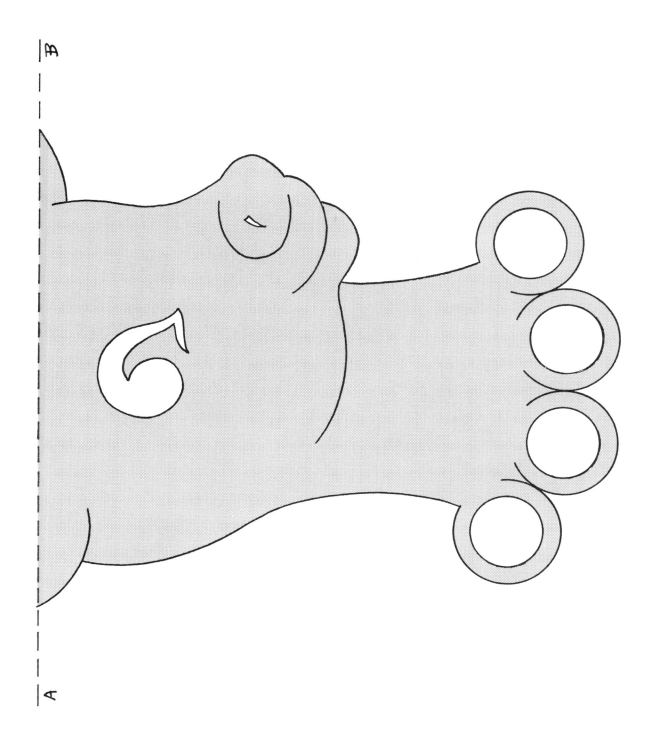

A

B

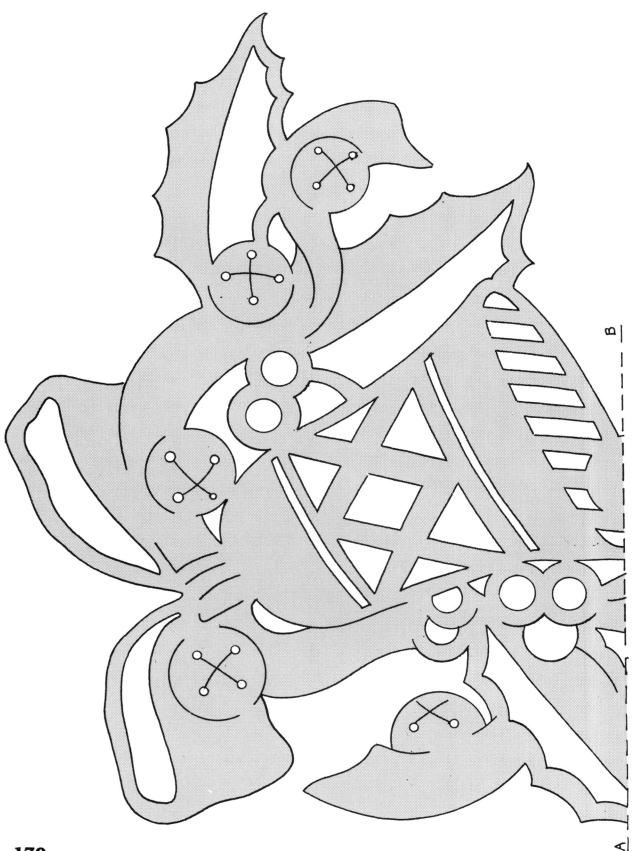

Plywood, ¹⁄₄″ thick, was used for this wall hanging.

A

B

Wall or trivet design. Cut from any available thickness.

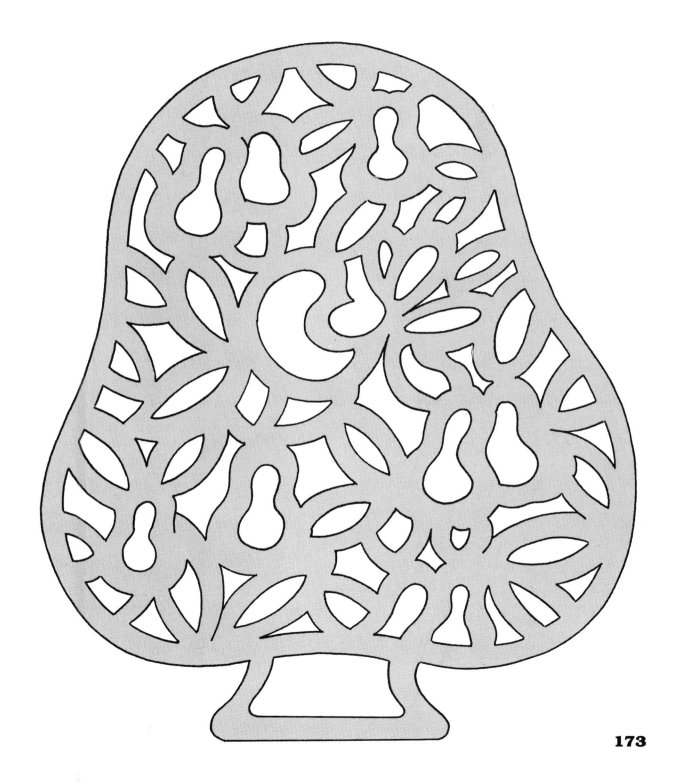

173

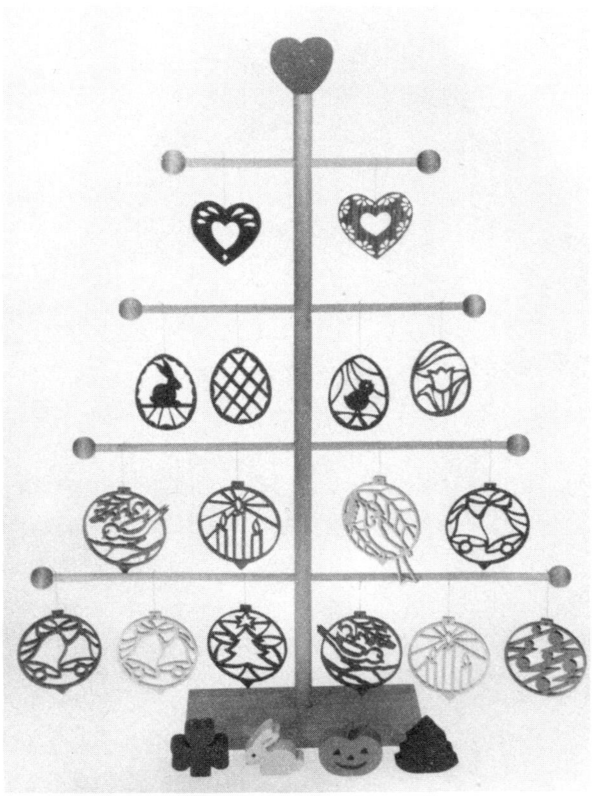

Ornament tree with interchangeable top decorations for various holidays.

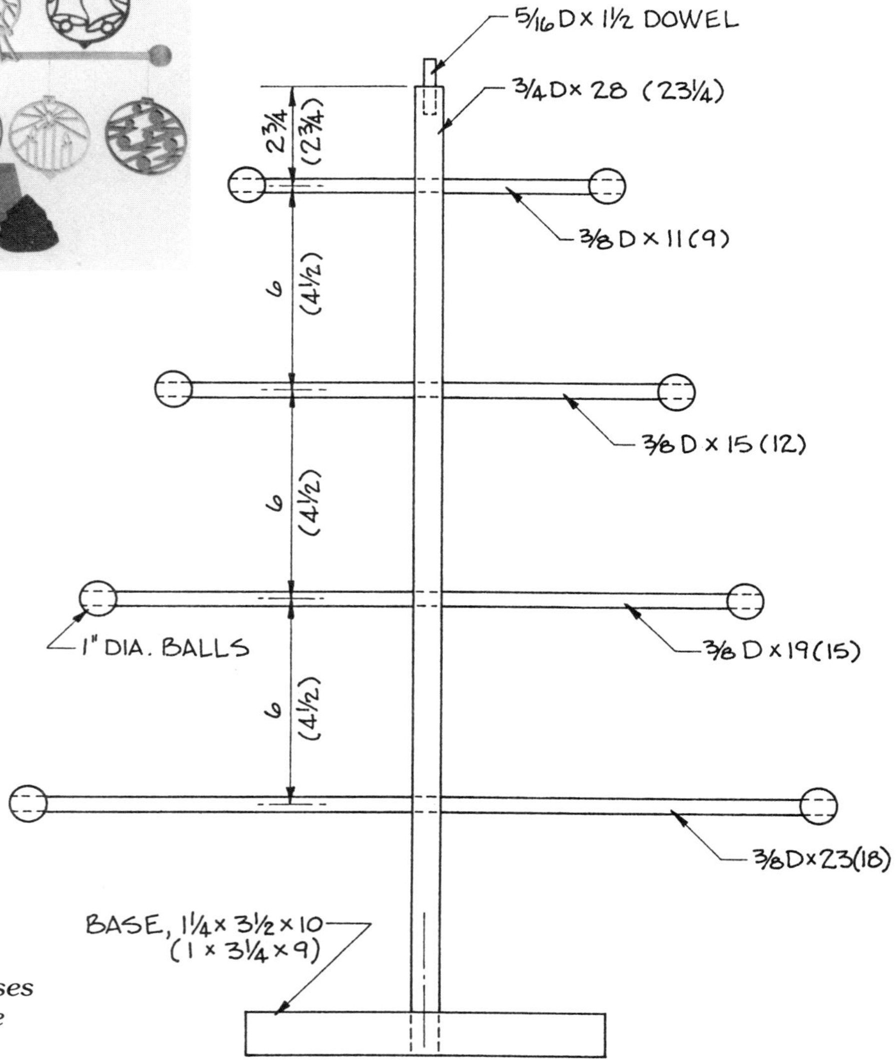

5/16D x 1½ DOWEL
¾D x 28 (23¼)
2¾ (2¾)
6 (4½)
6 (4½)
6 (4½)
⅜D x 11 (9)
⅜D x 15 (12)
1" DIA. BALLS
⅜D x 19 (15)
⅜D x 23 (18)
BASE, 1¼ x 3½ x 10
(1 x 3¼ x 9)

Ornament tree construction details, in your choice of two sizes. Dimensions in parentheses are for making the smaller size tree shown in the color section.

Patterns for interchangeable top decorations of the ornament tree.

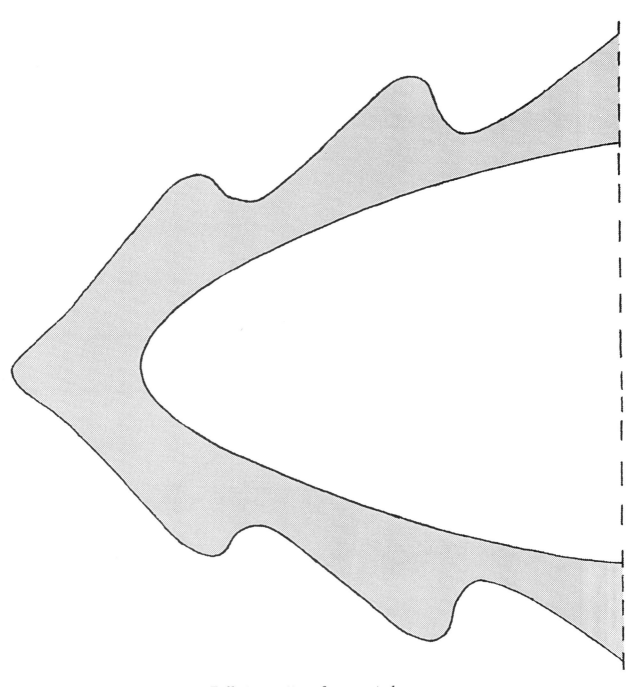

Full-size pattern for a routed Christmas tree tray.

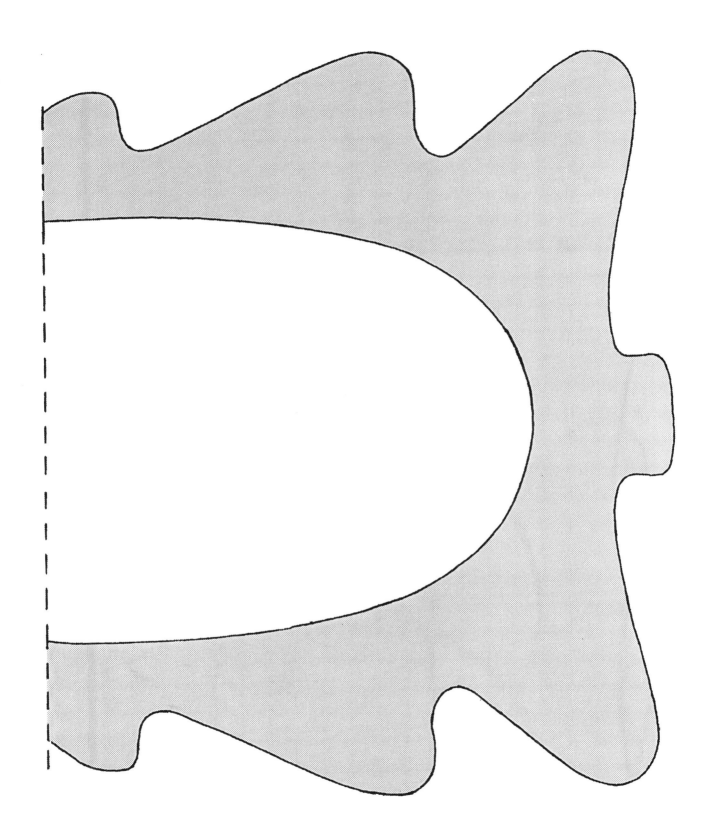

Basic setup for routing the tray recess. The pattern is attached to the ¾-inch (or thicker) by 8½-inch by 13½-inch wood blank with double-faced tape.

The routing operation. Note the work is placed on a routing mat that eliminates the need for any mechanical clamping devices.

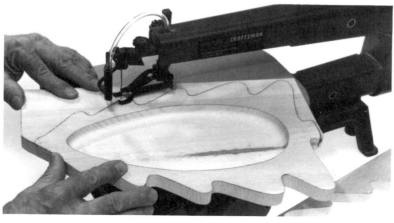

Once the inside is routed away, saw out the profile on the scroll saw. With the router, round over all outside edges (top and bottom), sand, and finish as desired.

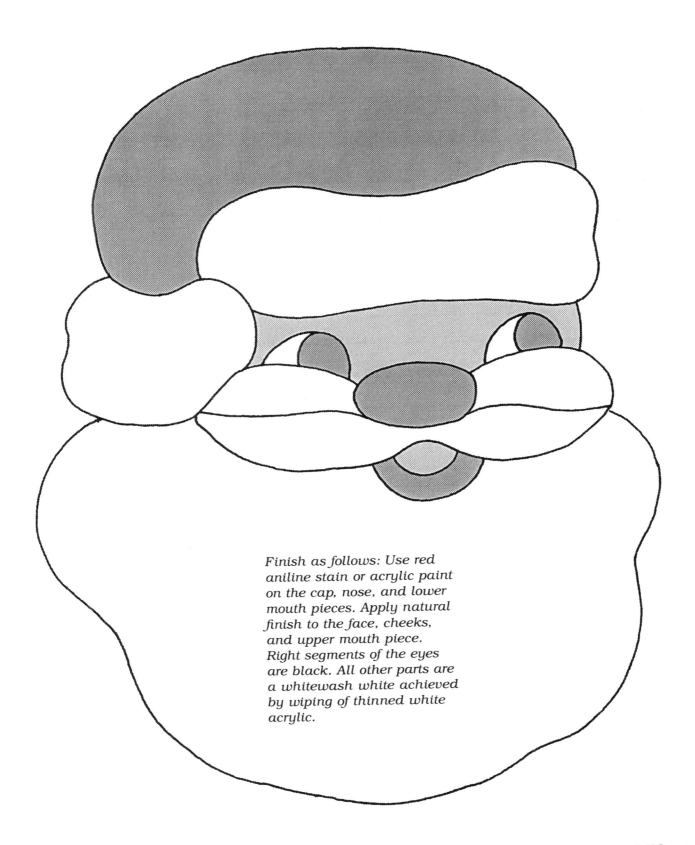

Finish as follows: Use red
aniline stain or acrylic paint
on the cap, nose, and lower
mouth pieces. Apply natural
finish to the face, cheeks,
and upper mouth piece.
Right segments of the eyes
are black. All other parts are
a whitewash white achieved
by wiping of thinned white
acrylic.

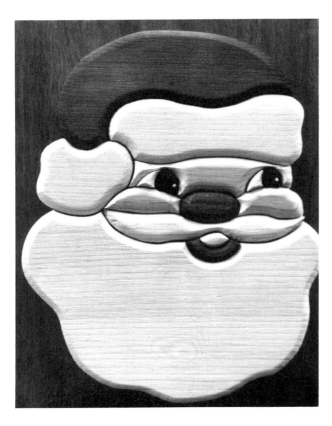

Segmented Santa wall plaque. Cut the pattern into individual pieces, stain or paint each part, and reassemble by gluing to a thin backing.

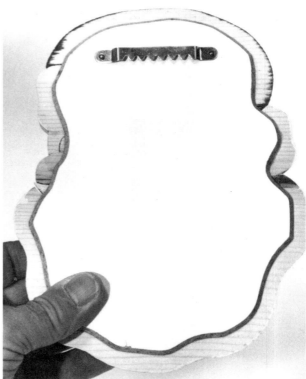

Back view of the segmented Santa face. Note that the backing is sawn smaller than the face profile. The backing is also bevel-sawn at approximately 30–35 degrees.

Scroll-sawing the various segments of the Santa face from ¾-inch-thick pine. It is best to orientate the pattern on the wood so the grain direction will be horizontal or in line with Santa's mustache.

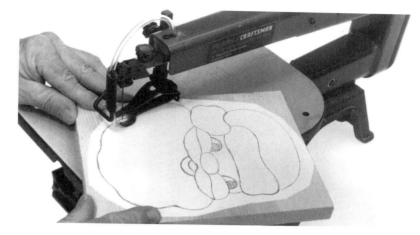

Rounding over the edges of the individual pieces. Note the use of the router pad, which eliminates the need for clamping. Another piece helps to support the router, keeping it from tipping. The edges of the very small parts should be rounded by hand using a rasp or knife and sandpaper.

A ¼-inch-radius corner-rounding bit and the router set-up for rounding over small parts. This custom sub-base made of clear plastic (or plywood) with minimal clearance around the bit replaces the factory sub-base.

Preparing the backing. The actual backing is cut about ¼ to ⅜ inch smaller than this initial outline being marked out here. Once cut, the individual parts are glued onto it, but after each piece is stained or painted.

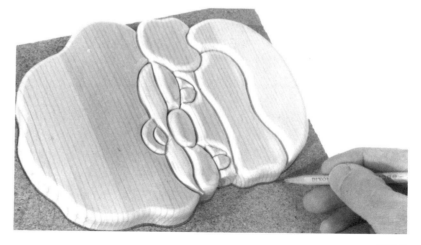

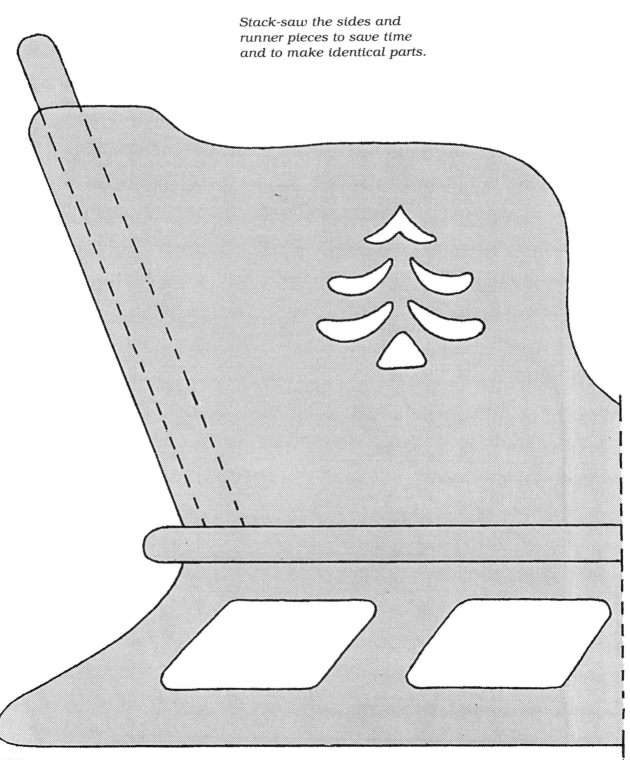

Stack-saw the sides and runner pieces to save time and to make identical parts.

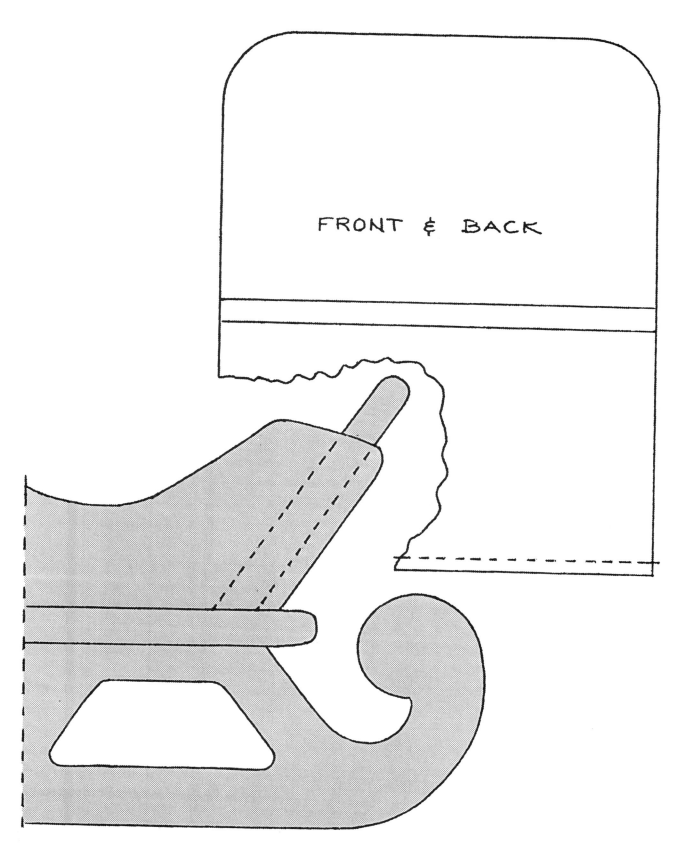

FRONT & BACK

Christmas sleigh made in two sizes. The large sleigh is double the size of the patterns as given here. Use ³⁄₈-inch-thick stock for the small sleigh, and ³⁄₄-inch-thick stock for the large one.

Optional dadoes for the front and back make for good construction and easier assembly. Cut dadoes to a depth equal to ¹⁄₃ of the stock thickness. If not using dado construction, the front and back patterns must be reduced accordingly in size: ¹⁄₄ inch less for the small sleigh and ¹⁄₂ inch less in total size for the large sleigh.

Rounding-over the edges of the small sleigh's runners on a router table. Use a corner-rounding bit with a ¹⁄₈-inch or ³⁄₁₆-inch radius on this and all other parts of the small-size sleigh.

Rounding-over the runners of the large-size sleigh with a hand-held router. Use a ⁵⁄₁₆-inch- or ³⁄₈-inch-radius corner-rounding bit.

Stop the round-over cuts short of the dadoes, as shown.

Making the pierced tree design cuts on the scroll saw.

Making a test assembly of the back and/or front to sides. Note: It's recommended to stain all pieces before final assembly.

Nail the bottom of the sides and then mount the runners by toe-nailing from the inside, as shown.

Additional Power Tool Accessories

Model 9 25172
Foot Pedal is a convenient accessory for foot-controlled on—off switch. Recommended for use with scroll saw to free the hands to guide the work piece.

Model 9 2573
Letter and Number Kit is a router accessory for engraving block-style letters. This kit is available at Sears. Router guide bushings are included. Letters are 2½" and 1½" high.

Rout-A-Copier
Model 9 25126
Available in Sears Power and Hand Tool Catalog.
Use Craftsman plunge routers to copy any drawing or letter in wood 1 to 1 (full size).

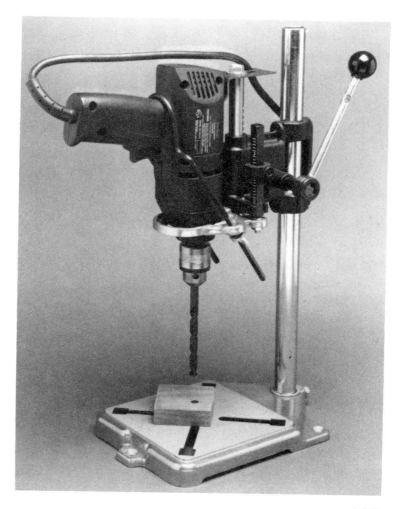

Drill Press Stand
Model 9 25921
Convert any Craftsman ¼- or ⅜-inch electric hand drill into a drill press for easy, accurate drilling.

Recommended Books

Carving Large Birds. Spielman and renowned woodcarver Bill Dehos show how to carve a fascinating array of large birds. All of the tools and basic techniques that are used are discussed in depth, and hundreds of photos, illustrations, and patterns are provided for carving graceful swans, majestic eagles, comical-looking penguins, a variety of owls, and scores of other birds. Oversized. 16 pages in full color. 192 pages.

Carving Wild Animals: Life-Size Wood Figures. Spielman and renowned woodcarver Bill Dehos show how to carve more than 20 magnificent creatures of the North American wild. A cougar, black bear, prairie dog, squirrel, raccoon, and fox are some of the life-size animals included. Step-by-step, photo-filled instructions and multiple-view patterns, plus tips on the use of tools, wood selection, finishing, and polishing, help you bring each animal to life. Oversized. Over 300 photos. 16 pages in full color. 240 pages.

Classic Fretwork Scroll Saw Patterns. With over 140 imaginative patterns inspired by and derived from mid- to late-nineteenth-century scroll-saw masters, this new book covers nearly 30 categories of patterns and includes a brief review of scroll-saw techniques and how to work with patterns. The patterns include ornamental numbers and letters, beautiful birds, signs, wall pockets, silhouettes, a sleigh, jewelry boxes, toy furniture, and more. 192 pages.

Gluing & Clamping. A thorough, up-to-date examination of one of the most critical steps in woodworking. Spielman explores the features of every type of glue—from traditional animal-hide glues to the newest epoxies—the clamps and tools needed, the bonding properties of different wood species, safety tips, and all techniques from edge-to-edge and end-to-end gluing to applying plastic laminates. Also included is a glossary of terms. Over 500 illustrations. 256 pages.

Making Country-Rustic Wood Projects. Hundreds of photos, patterns, and detailed scaled drawings reveal construction methods, woodworking techniques, and Spielman's professional secrets for making indoor and outdoor furniture in the distinctly attractive Country-Rustic style. Covered are all aspects of furniture making from choosing the best wood for the job to texturing smooth boards. Among the dozens of projects are mailboxes, cabinets, shelves, coffee tables, weather vanes, doors, panelling, plant stands, and many other durable and economical pieces. 400 illustrations. 4 pages in full color. 164 pages.

Making Wood Decoys. A clear step-by-step approach to the basics of decoy carving. This book is abundantly illustrated with closeup photos for designing, selecting, and obtaining woods; tools; feather detailing; painting; and finishing of decorative and working decoys. Six different professional decoy artists are featured. Photo gallery (4 pages in full color) along with numerous detailed plans for various popular decoys. 160 pages.

188

Making Wood Signs. Craftsman Model 25130. Designing, selecting woods and tools, and every process through finishing are clearly covered. Hand-carved, power-carved, routed, and sandblasted processes in small to huge signs are presented. Fool-proof guides for professional letters and ornaments. Hundreds of photos (4 pages in full color). Lists sources for supplies and special tooling.

Realistic Decoys. Spielman and master carver Keith Bridenhagen reveal their successful techniques for carving, feather texturing, painting, and finishing wood decoys. Details that you can't find elsewhere—anatomy, attitudes, markings, and the easy step-by-step approach to perfect delicate procedures—make this book invaluable. Includes listings for contests, shows, and sources of tools and supplies. 274 closeup photos, 28 in color. 224 pages.

Router Basics. With over 200 closeup step-by-step photos and drawings, this valuable overview will guide the new owner as well as provide a spark to owners for whom the router isn't the tool they turn to most often. Covers all the basic router styles, along with how-it-works descriptions of all its major features. Includes sections on bits and accessories as well as square-cutting and trimming, case and furniture routing, cutting circles and arcs, template and freehand routing, and using the router with a router table. 128 pages.

Router Handbook. Craftsman Model 25184. With nearly 600 illustrations of every conceivable bit, attachment, jig, and fixture, plus every possible operation, this definitive guide has revolutionized router applications. It begins with safety and maintenance tips, then forges ahead into all aspects of dovetailing, free-handing, advanced duplication, and more. Details for over 50 projects are included. 224 pages.

Router Jigs & Techniques. A practical encyclopedia of information, covering the lattest equipment to use with your router, it describes all the newest of commercial routing machines, along with jigs, bits, and other aids and devices. The book not only provides invaluable tips on how to determine the router and bits best suited to your needs, but tells you how to get the most out of your equipment once it is bought. Over 800 photos and illustrations. 384 pages.

Scroll Saw Basics. This overview features more than 275 illustrations covering basic techniques and accessories. Sections include types of saw, features, selection of blades, safety, and how to use patterns. A half-dozen patterns are included to help the scroll saw user get started. Basic cutting techniques are covered, including inside cuts, bevel cuts, stack-sawing, and others. 128 pages.

Scroll Saw Fretwork Techniques & Projects. This book offers a study in the historical development of fretwork, as well as the tools, techniques, materials, and project styles that have evolved over the past 130 years. Every intricate turn and cut is explained with over 550 step-by-step photos and illustrations. Patterns for all 32 projects are shown in full color. The book also covers some modern scroll-sawing machines as well as current state-of-the-art fretwork and fine scroll-sawing techniques. 232 pages.

Scroll Saw Handbook. Craftsman Model 25186. This companion volume to *Scroll Saw Pattern Book* covers the essentials of this versatile tool, including the basics (how scroll saws work, blades to use, etc.) and the advantages and disadvantages of the general types and specific brand-name models available on the market. All cutting techniques are detailed, including compound and bevel sawing, making inlays, reliefs, and recesses, cutting metals and other nonwoods, and marquetry. There's even a section on transferring patterns to wood! Over 500 illustrations. 256 pages.

Scroll Saw Pattern Book. This companion book to *Scroll Saw Handbook* contains over 450 workable patterns for making wall plaques, refrigerator magnets, candle holders, pegboards, jewelry, ornaments, shelves, brackets, picture frames, signboards, and many more projects. Beginners and experienced scroll saw users alike will find something to intrigue and challenge them. 256 pages.

Scroll Saw Puzzle Patterns. 80 full-size patterns for jigsaw puzzles, standup puzzles, and inlay puzzles. With meticulous attention to detail, Patrick and Patricia Spielman provide instruction and step-by-step photos, along with tips on tools and wood selections, for making standup puzzles in the shape of dinosaurs, camels, hippopotamuses, alligators—even a family of elephants! Inlay puzzle patterns include basic shapes, numbers, an accurate piece-together map of the United States, and a host of other colorful educational and enjoyable games for children. 8 pages of color. 256 pages.

Sharpening Basics. This overview goes well beyond the "basics" to become a major up-to-date reference work featuring more than 300 detailed illustrations (mostly photos) to explain every facet of tool sharpening. Sections include bench sharpening tools, sharpening machines, and safety. Chapters cover cleaning tools and sharp-

ening all sorts of tools including chisels, plane blades (irons), hand knives, carving tools, turning tools, drill and boring tools, router and shaper tools, jointer and planer knives, drivers and scrapers, and, of course, saws. 144 pages.

Spielman's Original Scroll Saw Patterns. 262 full-size patterns that don't appear elsewhere feature teddy bears, dinosaurs, sports figures, dancers, cowboy cutouts, Christmas ornaments, and dozens more. Fretwork patterns are included for a Viking ship, framed cutouts, wall-hangers, key-chain miniatures, jewelry, self-decoration, and much more. Hundreds of step-by-step photos and drawings show how to flop, repeat, and crop each design for thousands of variations. 4 pages of color. 228 pages.

Weekend Wood Projects. Craftsman Model 25128. Contains 62 original projects complete with detailed information on Rotary Power Tools and their accessories as well as other power tool accessories such as a drill press stand, foot pedal, and a letter and number kit. 192 pages.

Working Green Wood with PEG. Covers every process for making beautiful, inexpensive projects from green wood without cracking, splitting, or warping. Hundreds of clear photos and drawings show every step from obtaining the raw wood through shaping, treating, and finishing your PEG-treated projects. 175 unusual project ideas. Lists supply sources. 160 pages.

Index